FOCUS ON
BLOW-UP

John Allen

FILM FOCUS

Ronald Gottesman and Harry M. Geduld
General Editors

THE FILM FOCUS SERIES PRESENTS THE BEST THAT HAS BEEN WRITTEN ABOUT THE ART OF FILM AND THE MEN WHO CREATED IT. COMBINING CRITICISM WITH HISTORY, BIOGRAPHY, AND ANALYSIS OF TECHNIQUE, THE VOLUMES IN THE SERIES EXPLORE THE MANY DIMENSIONS OF THE FILM MEDIUM AND ITS IMPACT ON MODERN SOCIETY.

ROY HUSS *is Assistant Professor of English at Queens College of the City University of New York. A member of the American Federation of Film Societies, he is an addicted moviegoer and broadcaster about the film experience.*

FOCUS ON

BLOW-UP

edited by
ROY HUSS

A SPECTRUM BOOK

Prentice-Hall, Inc.
Englewood Cliffs, N. J.

PRENTICE-HALL INTERNATIONAL, INC. (*London*)
PRENTICE-HALL OF AUSTRALIA, PTY. LTD. (*Sydney*)
PRENTICE-HALL OF CANADA, LTD. (*Toronto*)
PRENTICE-HALL OF INDIA PRIVATE LIMITED (*New Delhi*)
PRENTICE-HALL OF JAPAN, INC. (*Tokyo*)

for
Sheila

CONTENTS

Blow-Up: Cast and Credits   *xiii*

Introduction
    by Roy Huss   *1*

Antonioni in the English Style: A Day on the Set   *7*

The Blow-Up: Sorting Things Out
    by Charles Thomas Samuels   *13*

REVIEWS

No Antoniennui
    by Andrew Sarris   *31*

Blow-Up
    by F. A. Macklin   *36*

Blow-Up
    by Carey Harrison   *39*

Blow-Up
    by Hubert Meeker   *46*

The Road to Damascus: *Blow-Up*
    by Jean Clair   *53*

The Blow-Up
    by Max Kozloff   *58*

ESSAYS

Three Encounters with *Blow-Up*
    by *Arthur Knight*   67

A Year with *Blow-Up*: Some Notes
    by *Stanley Kauffmann*   70

Antonioni in Transit
    by *Marsha Kinder*   78

Blow-Up: Antonioni and the Mod World
    by *James F. Scott*   89

Cool Times
    by *T. J. Ross*   98

Isolation and Make-Believe in *Blow-Up*
    by *George Slover*   107

Blow-Up: From the Word to the Image
    by *John Freccero*   116

Synopsis   129

Outline   131

Three Sequences from *Blow-Up*: A Shot Analysis
    by *Kay Hines*   135

Filmography   141

Bibliography   146

APPENDIX

Blow-Up
  by Julio Cortázar   *151*

From Cortázar to Antonioni: Study of an Adaptation
  by Henry Fernández   *163*

BLOW-UP

Metro-Goldwyn-Mayer, Films, Inc. (16mm, non-theatrical)

PRODUCTION COMPANY	Bridge Films (Carlo Ponti) for MGM
EXECUTIVE PRODUCER	Pierre Rouve
PRODUCTION MANAGER	Donald Toms
DIRECTOR	Michelangelo Antonioni
ASSISTANT DIRECTOR	Claude Watson
SCRIPT	Michelangelo Antonioni and Tonino Guerra, based on a short story by Julio Cortázar
DIALOGUE	Edward Bond
DIRECTOR OF PHOTOGRAPHY	Carlo Di Palma
EDITOR	Frank Clarke
SETS	Assheton Gorton
PHOTOGRAPHIC MURALS	John Cowan
MUSIC	Herbert Hancock; "Stroll On" featured by The Yardbirds
COSTUMES	Jocelyn Rickards
TIME: 111 MINUTES	

Filmed on location in London and at the MGM Studios, Boreham Wood; April–August 1966. First shown in New York, December 1966. Grand Prix (Palme d'Or) at Cannes Film Festival, 1967; Paris, 24 May 1967; Prize of the International Federation of Cine-Clubs.

CAST

Jane	VANESSA REDGRAVE
Thomas	DAVID HEMMINGS
Patricia	SARAH MILES
Ron	PETER BOWLES
Models	VERUSHKA, JILL KENNINGTON, PEGGY MOFFITT, ROSALEEN MURRAY, ANN NORMAN, MELANIE HAMPSHIRE
Teenagers	JANE BIRKIN, GILLIAN HILLS
Antique Dealer	HARRY HUTCHINSON
Painter	JOHN CASTLE
Antique Shop Owner	SUSAN BRODERICK
Fashion Editor	MARY KHAL
Jane's Lover	RONAN O'CASEY
Receptionist	TSAI CHIN

FOCUS ON
BLOW-UP

Introduction
by ROY HUSS

Probably no film of the last decade has created such a wide range of responses as *Blow-Up*. While some reviewers were eager to apply their electric kool-aid acid-test kits to determine whether an Italian "tourist," no matter how celebrated, could really capture an ambience as complex as the mod subculture of London, other more seasoned movie buffs—entrenched in their bias for thrillers since the good old days of Monogram—settled back into their comfortable notion that here at last was a film that was worthy of Hitchcock, although its un-Hitchcockian nudity and sex and unsolved mysteries should have given them some pause. At cocktail parties the question of whether Antonioni did in fact depict a murder and show a real—rather than an hallucinatory—corpse continued to reverberate like a wave of echoes. All will perhaps be put to rights someday when, as *TV Guide* suggests, the "edited for television" version replaces the girls of the celebrated nude romp with two loveable, but sensual, cocker spaniels, and materializes the invisible tennis ball inscribed with the name of the murderer.

While interpretations became more diversified and critics more polarized, Fate conspired to add a new note of discord to *Blow-Up*'s reception. The film arrived in the United States—its title telegraphically reduced from *The Blow-Up*—just as a new system of film ratings was going into effect. The widely touted "liberalized" policy of the Motion Picture Association of America—namely to make heretofore censorable films more accessible to mature audiences by creating a special X-rated category—was immediately short-circuited by Antonioni's unexpected boldness. Although he allowed *Blow-Up*'s two female principals, Sarah Miles and Vanessa Redgrave, to display their nudity with modesty (the former by having her body completely covered by the man in an intercourse scene; the latter by keeping her arms coyly folded over her naked breasts in an abortive sex encounter),

1

he caused two young unknown starlets playing the roles of aspiring models to frolic uninhibitedly before his camera, one of them even offering a fleeting glimpse of pudendum. While the MPAA pondered hairline distinctions between art and morality, and deliberated whether the film should be certified under the new code, Antonioni made it known that he adamantly opposed any deletions, although he later consented to a few. The reaction by Metro-Goldwyn-Mayer, the film's producing company, became *"noli me tangere"*: it simply evaded the issue by releasing the unlicensed film under the name of a subsidiary. Meanwhile, *Blow-Up* quietly took first prize at the Cannes Film Festival, and then, with more fanfare, the award for the best film of the year given in New York by the newly formed National Society of Film Critics.

Throughout 1967, the *New York Times* recorded such disparate and remote earth tremors as the attack by Bosley Crowther on the MPAAs disapproval, the banning of the film in Catholic Buenos Aires, and the screening of it as a moral exemplum by a Protestant church in Brooklyn. Since then, the appearance of far more sexually graphic films, such as *I Am Curious (Yellow)* and *Censorship in Denmark,* has allowed the dust to settle on *Blow-Up* as a *cause célèbre*. This means that at last we can concentrate on the film's purely aesthetic qualities— those which have prompted more than one serious critic to regard it as a modern classic.

Although the creator of a classic may rely on the conventions of his genre, he simultaneously transcends them. Like George Bernard Shaw, Antonioni is well versed in ways to capitalize on forms of expression most in vogue (for Antonioni, in this case, the murder mystery; for Shaw, the historical romance and the "well-made" play). But, also like Shaw, Antonioni is skilful in undercutting stock expectations by diverting the action into unanticipated byways. In *Blow-Up* he has found a way to dramatize the unspoken thoughts that release a concatenation of events. Beneath the surface glitter of mod life and the little crises of work and play that seem so easily discharged in such minor activities as pot parties, rock sessions, sexual flirtations, and tennis games lie the hypnotic never-to-be-resolved questions of how the illusion of art relates to the experience of life and how the experiences of both life and art relate to death. In this film, Antonioni has suggested a central mystery at the core of the merely mysterious.

Whether or not one agrees that *Blow-Up* deserves to be called a film classic is perhaps ultimately unimportant. What is clear is that it will continue to fascinate serious moviegoers. This is probably because it rests firmly on what I call the three keystones of film art— three ingredients that have been intrinsic to it from the beginning.

These are the ease and gracefulness with which it treats the real world as malleable, while seeming to faithfully document it; the success with which it spatializes time and abstract thought; and the degree to which it is able to enlist the detached-but-involved interest of the eavesdropper and the voyeur.

As to the first, we are indisputably descendants of the frequenters of the nickelodeons who delighted not only in seeing real trains pulling into real stations on the screen, but also in knowing that the filmmaker could, as if by magic, bend this kind of simple movement to his will—accelerate or retard it, or at least show it in different ways from different angles. Antonioni has always avoided a self-conscious display of his mastery of the medium, but in *Blow-Up* he enters a new dimension. By transforming Cortazár's amateur photographer into a professional one, a would-be transcriber of life as well as an artificer of fashion, he makes the aesthetics of documentary filmmaking itself one of the key themes of the film. Whether the photographer's camera has created, distorted, or merely recorded reality becomes a question of technique as well as one of psychology and epistemology.

Concerning the second keystone of cinematic art—the way in which the film medium best reveals time and emotion through the dynamics of space-play, I refer the reader to the classic essay on this subject by the brilliant art historian Erwin Panofsky.[1] Briefly summarized, Panofsky's article argues that the primitive artists connected with film's "folk-art" beginnings were essentially correct in feeling that drama for the film medium meant movement—not movement bound by the exigencies of limited setting or by the range of gestures of performers, as in the theatre, but movement born of the constant shifting of spaces and planes, of light and shadow. When involving actors, a filmed sequence made the most dynamic use of space when the threat of a confrontation exploded into a frantic pursuit, as it did in the great locomotive chase in Keaton's *The General*.

In the more sophisticated cinema of today—fraught as it is with ideological and psychological subleties—the use of the chase to spatialize dramatic tensions and inner states of mind may not be so obvious. But in the best films it is present in at least some transformed or rarified state. In *Blow-Up,* as in *Marienbad* and *The Seventh Seal,* we see it as a very cerebral, but nevertheless spatially oriented, kind of pursuit—a pursuit of a moment in time that epitomizes some crisis of identification or of self-awareness, and that takes us through endless corridors (*Marienbad*) or over medieval landscapes (*The Seventh Seal*).

[1] Reprinted in T. J. Ross, ed., *Film and the Liberal Arts* (New York: Holt, Rinehart & Winston, Inc., 1970), pp. 375–94.

In *Blow-Up,* as in these other films, the search for self rightly takes the form of a physical quest, in which the protagonist moves successively through a park, in and out of a jungle of photographic equipment, among crowds of hostile and indifferent people. However, here too Antonioni enriches an artistic element by actually making it a subject for study: he not only dramatizes the photographer's quest by choreographing his position with relation to people, objects, and background, but he also allows him, as artist-creator, to "spatialize" dramas of his own: to photograph the lovers from different angles and distances in the park and to arrange fashion models in front of and behind smoked-glass screens in order to give odd perspectives to his tableaux.

The third keystone upon which film art makes a bid for our involvement—that of appealing to the voyeur and eavesdropper in all of us—also goes back to its origins, to the lure of the peep show. When the prototype of the modern film buff forsook the eyepiece of the mutoscope and the kinetoscope for the darkened auditorium of the nickelodeon, he made the ultimate commitment to voyeurism that filmgoers have made ever since—acceptance of a womb-like blackness from which to witness, undisturbed and unobserved, intimate scenes that are heightened by the luminescence of projection. *Blow-Up* certainly owes its popularity in part to how it caters to this basic impulse. Antonioni's camera allows us to witness an orgy and several abortive seductions, and, as one critic remarks, lasciviously watches with us from a low angle as the two teenagers, their behinds straining the material of their tight mini-skirts, climb the stairs to the photographer's studio. Yet as before, Antonioni carries his convention a step further: he not only makes us voyeurs but he also studies the act of voyeurism itself. A fascinating fact of the film is that some of the photographer's observations come when he is, like a film audience, encapsulated by darkness: in his darkroom developing the blow-ups (one of the prints even resembling an illuminated movie screen as he goes behind it), or in the park at night viewing the body (the cadaver almost seeming to be projected by the garish light of the neon sign).

Sooner or later an artist who is both serious and prolific produces a work that has as its subject the very medium in which the artist himself is working, or at least an allegory of the artist's relation to that medium. Shakespeare and Ibsen dramatized this theme at the end of their careers in *The Tempest* and in *When We the Dead Awaken.* Thomas Mann and W. B. Yeats explored it throughout their creative years. In the film world, Bergman dealt with it tangentially in *Sawdust and Tinsel (The Naked Night)* and later in *Persona,* while Fellini treated it exhaustively in *8½.*

  Blow-Up is Antonioni's contribution to the subject of the artist's involvement with his medium. In fact, in many ways, it is a filmmaker's film: Antonioni's fascination with the art and craft of still photography—a sister art to cinematography—shines through at every point. He acknowledges this attraction in his brief foreword to the published Italian version of the screenplay:

> The idea for *Blow-Up* came to me while reading a short story by Julio Cortázar. I was not so much interested in the events as in the technical aspects of photography. I discarded the plot and wrote a new one in which the equipment itself assumed a different weight and significance.[2]

The filmmaker's involvement with his own craft is revealed in *Blow-Up* in one of the most spell-binding sequences of cinematic art— the one in which the photographer enlarges the series of photographs of the man and woman in the park. In a *tour de force* of artistic transcendence, Antonioni uses his own camera to compel the still-photographer to create a motion picture of the crime—a parallel to the photo-animation that occurs in the mind of the amateur photographer in Cortázar's story. In the beginning of the sequence, Hemmings merely resembles a film editor as he rearranges his "shots" in their proper or most revealing sequence, occasionally inserting close-ups (i.e., blow-ups) to produce what a film director would call Vanessa Redgrave's "eye-line shots"—representations of what she is gazing at off-screen. But it is only when Antonioni begins to pan his own camera over the series of photos—sometimes dollying in on one of them for a "close-up"; once following Hemmings behind a translucent enlargement hanging on the drying-line for a "reverse angle shot" of the photographed park scene—that he begins to activate the series of stills into a kind of motion picture. By finally erasing the image of the photographer himself from the screen, Antonioni reveals even more decisively his directorial presence and control.

  I hope that my account of the spectrum of public reaction to *Blow-Up* and my hints at the complexity of the form and meaning of the film have prepared the reader for the range of criticism and inter-

[2] Foreword to *Blow-Up,* 2nd ed. (Torino: Giulio Einaudi, 1968), p. 7. My translation.

pretation in the articles I have included in this volume. Some of the more circumspect pieces, like those of Samuels and Kinder, are concerned with the question of whether Antonioni has, with *Blow-Up*, merely forged another link in his chain of preoccupations with *tedium vitae* and the impossibilities of communication, or whether his unexpected change of venue and stepped-up rhythm of editing signal a radical departure. Several of the authors explore this question either by analyzing Antonioni's experiments with color (Sarris and Kozloff), or by examining his almost iconographical and symbolic use of objects and blackgrounds (Clair). Others, most notably Freccero, push the implications even further and wonder if perhaps Antonioni has begun in *Blow-Up* to create a new cinematic language. Still other writers examine the film more thematically as they investigate its engagement with mod life and pop art (Ross); its involvement with the sexual mores of present-day youth (Slover); its preoccupation with the more perennial themes of violence, death, and love (Scott); its flirtation with what more than one critic called a Pirandellian concern for reality and illusion.

The remainder of the material that I have selected will, I hope, further encourage the reader to re-assess his own reactions to the film. By presenting an eye-witness report of Antonioni at work on the set of *Blow-Up*, together with the remarks he made to his guest observer, I have tried to place all of us within earshot of the oracle himself. By reprinting in its entirety the Cortázar story upon which Antonioni loosely based his film alongside a study of the adaptation, I hope to give the reader a chance for an unprecedented insight into Antonioni's craftsmanship and imagination. And, finally, by providing a detailed shot analysis of three of the film's most exciting sequences, along with stills of these and other highlights, I have tried to re-awaken the reader's most vivid memories of the film—an experience that he can hope to surpass only by seeing it again.

Antonioni in the English Style:
A Day on the Set

. . . "Blow-Up" must be seen as the interpretation of an era, an age that is carefree on the surface, but terrifying in its depths. The film is set in a city subject to the caprices of fashion, gaudy with "pop" colors and populated by crowds of young people who eagerly seek escape from the daily humdrum by getting "stoned" on LSD.

Antonioni wrote "Blow-Up" with the help of both his faithful collaborator Tonino Guerra and the young English dramatist Edward Bond, whose violent play "Saved," now suppressed by the censor, provoked a scandal last winter. Bond has had an important role in editing the dialogue of "Blow-Up," but has not contributed as much as Guerra to the elaboration of the scenario. The violence which often surfaces in this film cannot be compared to that which triggers the events shaping the plot of "Saved." Bond has depicted a violence that is visible and physical. Antonioni makes us sensible to a violence that stimulates feelings and ideas. He comments on this in a single phrase: "It often happens that I experience fragmentary feelings before the experiences themselves take hold."

The principal part, that of the photographer, is interpreted by David Hemmings, a stage actor who is not too familiar with the cinema (his screen debut: Clive Donner's "Some People"). Vanessa Redgrave and Sarah Miles play the two female roles. "Blow-Up" is being shot in color under the supervision of the chief director of photography of "The Red Desert," Carlo Di Palma. The British "pop" group known as The Animals will provide the musical portion.

At the opening of "Blow-Up" the camera discovers one of those clothes emporiums which drip with neon and border on Carnaby

Street, as it is being visited by Thomas, the photographer, his meddling camera clutched in his hand.[1] The whole film is realized in natural decor, exteriors and interiors alike.

By way of providing a set, Antonioni's employers—Metro-Goldwyn-Mayer—have rented a photographer's studio for the occasion. We are now inside Thomas' room: walls whitened with lime, a black ceiling. Gray furniture. A bright gray rug is spread out on a black floor. On the beams of the ceiling and on the walls hang enormous photographic enlargements in black and white. In these very coarse-grained images one can recognize the young woman of the park and her companion.

The atmosphere remains clear, fresh, and transparent, in spite of the overpowering heat generated by the floodlights.

In the studio, screens made of smoked glass six and a half feet high are set up. Photographers' models pose either behind or in front of these screens, and there, also, the film's characters interact with each other. For this drama Antonioni has intentionally conceived a setting that is poor in color, a universe of distorted images, of reflections. Behind the partitions of glass, reality seems to be in disorder [Plate III].

"I wish to re-create reality in an abstract form," Antonioni declares. "I put reality itself in question. This is an essential point with which the visual aspect of this film is concerned, given the fact that one of its principal themes is 'to see rightly, or else not to see the true value of things.' "

In MGMs temporary office, a motto is posted on one of the walls: "A shot a day keeps the producer away!"

Progress on "Blow-Up" is slow. Shooting began in May [1966] and in August some of the continuities still remain to be filmed. The film's director of production, Pierre Rouve, an Italian-Rumanian with sad eyes and a voice that becomes plaintive when he launches into his long tirades, reminds everyone of costs and of the number of shooting days that have come to be added to those originally planned. But: "Antonioni is a great artist. What can one do? We give him all the quiet, all the time, all the material he needs. In return, we hope of course to have a very good film." This confidence is completely mutual.

Antonioni's fastidiousness is well known. He is a perfectionist: with rapt attention he controls even the most minute details in the course of his work. He looks into the viewfinder more often than most other directors, and uses the cameraman's seat more than the framer does. In fact, Antonioni practically always decides the framing and composition of his images.

That afternoon they shoot only a single scene. The number of takes

---

[1] This sequence was obviously scrapped later [Editor's note].

increases to twenty-one before Antonioni declares himself totally satisfied.

He is concerned with one of the key scenes of the film: an encounter between Thomas, the photographer, and the wife of his best friend, Patricia, played by Sarah Miles. Scene all set up. Performers in profile. Exchanges of remarks, but to Sarah Miles falls the responsibility of conducting the game.

The worst enemy is the sound. "Blow-Up" is being shot in direct sound and the nonexistent soundproofing of the photographer's studio does not make the job easy. The din of the traffic threatens to drown out the text. The fourteenth take ends with a peal of bells from a church in the neighborhood. Hysterical laughter on the set.

The twentieth take comes off perfectly. It is then that the assistant director notices that someone from the working crew has modified a detail in the decor. In an instant a storm is let loose. Antonioni, in the height of rage and despair, cries out, "All London seems to be against me!"

The confiding scene between Thomas and Patricia is typical of the desperate and depressing tone of the film. Thomas and Patricia give the impression of living in doubt, a doubt that only deepens from day to day. They imagine that they are leading an absolutely free existence, whereas, in fact, they are two magnificent caged birds, prisoners of a whole web of ritualistic acts. They are in search of stable values in order to be able to live in a time marked by the negation of values and permanent instability. In the conversation, Patricia's replies betray her fear and her defeatism: "You must help me. In five years I shall come towards you—or you towards me—and then you will kill me. Everything would be so much simpler if I knew how to have only five years to live. I would organize my life; I would dedicate myself only to what is essential to it." [2]

"Blow-Up" is a story without a *denouement,* comparable in tone to those novels of the twenties in which writers like Scott Fitzgerald showed their distaste for life.

Antonioni has a tired look. He admits to sleeping badly during the shooting of his films. Moreover, the language barrier adds to his exhaustion. To be sure, Antonioni speaks a respectable English, but he prefers to give the more precise and detailed instructions for set-ups in French, leaving his interpreter to translate them. Snags in the translations sometimes cause misunderstandings and also devour precious minutes.

A little later in the photographer's studio: Sarah Miles is supposed

[2] Omitted from the final version [Editor's note].

to emit an embarrassed laugh after her previous reply, but Antonioni is not satisfied with her smile. He goes into a huddle with the translator, who has confused "gené" [embarrassed] with "genereux" [generous, or abundant]. The translator also tries to make his own personal point of view understood: "But this smile is a reaction that is quite British!" Antonioni: "I hope no one will say that 'Blow-Up' is a typically English film. But, at the same time, I hope that no one says it is Italian."

At first, the story of "Blow-Up" was to be set in Italy, but it proved to be impossible to do the shooting there.

"In the first place, a person like Thomas does not really exist in Italy. However, in England, those newspapers with heavy print that you find there use photographs like those I have captured in my film. Thomas is also about to become entangled in events which are easier to relate to London than to life in Rome or Milan. He has opted for the revolution which affects life, customs, and morality here in England, at least among the young artists, designers, advertising men, models or musicians who are inspired by the 'pop' movement. His existence is regulated like a ceremony, although he says he knows no law other than anarchy. I came to London last year, and I waited around a long time while Monica Vitti was filming 'Modesty Blaise.' I noticed then that London would be an ideal setting for a film like this. But I do not really intend to make a film about London. The same story could be shot in New York, perhaps also in Stockholm, and certainly in Paris."

For his exteriors, Antonioni perfers a pale gray sky to a frankly blue pastel one. He is trying to work out a scale of realistic tones for "Blow-Up" and has renounced certain effects obtained in "The Red Desert."

"During that time I worked a lot with a telephoto lens in order to get flattened perspectives, so that I could tie together people and objects and make them seem pasted one on top the other. Nothing like that this time. On the contrary, I have been trying to deepen the perspective, to put air between persons and things. The only time I used the telephoto lens was when circumstances forced me: for example, when I had to shoot right in the middle of a traffic jam. The greatest problem I have run into has been that of recreating the reality of violence. Color automatically embellishes and often sweetens that which, to the eye, seems harsh and aggressive."

In "Blow-Up," eroticism occupies a key place. But, often, the accent is on a cold, intellectual kind of sensuality. Exhibitionism and voyeurism are especially emphasized: the young woman of the park undresses and offers her body to the photographer in exchange for the negative which she is so anxious to recover; Thomas is a witness to intercourse between Patricia and her husband, and his presence as spectator seems to increase the young wife's excitement; finally, the film ends with a party that sinks into debauchery.

"The scabrous side of the film would surely have made it impossible to shoot it in Italy. Censorship has without a doubt become more tolerant in many parts of the world, but it remains firmly entrenched in Italy, the country which, remember, harbors the Holy See.

"In my film, there is for example a scene in the photographer's studio in which two young girls, less than twenty years old, disport themselves in a way that is especially provocative. They are completely nude. But that scene was not constructed for ogling. I believe I filmed it in a way that no one would judge obscene. This sequence is not erotic, any more than it is vulgar. It is fresh, light—and I venture to hope—funny. I cannot prevent anyone from finding a scabrous side, but I needed that scene in the film, and I did not wish to renounce it for fear of its not suiting others' tastes."

We might perhaps recall the sentence Antonioni wrote in the preface to one of his scenarios: "My films are documents not of a train of coherent ideas but of ideas which are born of the moment." He therefore refuses to speak of the preconceived notions he has put into the film to which, at the moment, he devotes all his time.

"It is impossible for me to analyze one of my creations before the work is completely finished. I am a maker of films, a man having certain ideas which I hope to be able to express with enough sincerity and clarity. As for knowing if it tells a story about our time, or, on the contrary, a story without any relevance to our world, I am incapable of deciding—at least as determined by the present phase of my work.

"When I really set myself to thinking about this film, I often stay awake all night, reflecting and taking notes. Soon the story, with its multiple possibilities, will fascinate me, and I will try to guess where its different implications could lead me. But now that I have arrived at a certain phase, I say to myself: let's continue by making the film itself. Frankly, I am not at all sure what I am in the middle of. All the same, I have a presentiment, because I am in on the secret.

"I believe in working in a way which is at once reflective and intuitive. For example, a few minutes ago, I isolated myself in order to reflect on the scene which would follow. I tried to put myself in the shoes of the principal character of the film, when he discovers the body. I walked over there, on the plot of grass, into the shadows, under the mysterious brightness of the neon sign. I approached the make-believe corpse and I truly identified with the film's protagonist. I was fully able to imagine his excitement, his emotions, the feelings that would be triggered by my hero's discovery of the body, the way he was going to conduct himself, to move, to react. This lasted only a minute or two. Then the rest of the equipment arrived, and my inspirations and sensations put out to sea."

THE BLOW-UP:
Sorting Things Out
by CHARLES THOMAS SAMUELS

. . . Some critics, notably Stanley Kauffmann and Ian Cameron, have accurately described Antonioni's effort to disentagle cinema from theater, but they have not perceived the radical lengths to which he has gone. Every important director, from popular artists like Hitchcock to serious *auteurs* like Kurosawa and Bergman, has exploited cinema's unique ability both to imprison the spectator in the lens's grip and to free him through speed and scope of movement; but Antonioni stands alone in making the visual image his fundamental mode of expression. He does not tell a story; he presents gestures and tableaux. He does not explore characters; he moves figures through a landscape. Yet, although his films are filled with things to look at, he does not shoot scenery.

To begin with: plot. Antonioni's plots are really antiplots, since his characters are chronically unable to engage in productive action. Thus, in *L'Avventura,* Claudia and Sandro cannot truly search for his lost fiancée because they cannot truly care whether she is found. In *La Notte,* the unhappily married protagonists accomplish nothing in their long, eventful day, while the lovers' appointment in *Eclipse* is never, so far as we can tell, kept. Giuliana, of *Red Desert,* performs the one significant act in Antonioni, but that is only a spiritual adjustment to the modern world. Plot suspense is utterly avoided; our desire for knowledge focuses on character.

But not on character as unique personage, with determinant past and significant future. Antonioni's people are simply what we see,

Reprinted with deletions and minor revisions from The American Scholar, *Winter 1967–68, pp. 120–31. Copyright © 1969 by Charles Thomas Samuels. Reprinted by permission of the author.*

which is why they are always defined by dead-end jobs. Sandro, once an architect, is now an appraiser; while Giovanni, in *La Notte,* is a writer who doubts the possibility of another book. The sensitive heroine of *Eclipse* is doomed to the soulless and the secondhand: her lover works for the stock exchange, while she translates for a living. Even Giuliana has a depleting job, that of full-time neurotic. Unlike characters in other works that are similarly focused, Antonioni's do not develop. Their stories show them assuming a role—Claudia becoming Sandro's lover—or understanding the roles they have always played— Sandro facing his emptiness.

Since Antonioni's characters do not really engage in action and do not radically change, their inward fixity calls for a new kind of film movement. Whereas most directors move your eye across the surface of the action, Antonioni tries to move your eye into its depths. For most directors, a close-up represents, as it were, the locus of event and dialogue. In Antonioni, events occur behind faces, which express themselves not in dialogue but in gesture: a flick of the eye, a grimace. Antonioni's close-ups must be "read." Furthermore, whereas most directors bombard the spectator with images or hurl him through space, Antonioni holds his eye in front of carefully composed scenes.

The last characteristic is the heart of Antonioni's method. A director who emphasizes action will photograph the background as an agent; as, for example, Hitchcock photographs the windshield wipers of Janet Leigh's car in *Psycho*: normal servants turned by the plot into menacing blades. A director who explores character will arrange the background into an "objective correlative"; as, for example, Fellini does in *8½.* Antonioni handles decor in neither way. In his films, the background does not enhance or reflect the foreground but rather interacts with and interprets it.

In his first important film, *L'Avventura,* the two main female characters are established by the simplest visual means: Anna, who has dark hair and scowls a great deal, represents withdrawal from society to which blond, always smiling Claudia is innocently attracted. In the film's second scene, Anna leaves Claudia inspecting a Roman square while she deliberately stages a test of her love for Sandro. As we watch Anna's face disgustedly receiving Sandro's caress, we see the nullity of their relationship and, since we shall later see the faces of Sandro and Claudia turning in the same erotic dance, we preview the essential anonymity of relationships in this world.

That Claudia is destined to replace her, Anna realizes when, with a smirk, she forces Claudia to wear her blouse in the subsequent yachting scene. This image must come back to our minds when, at Taormina, Claudia playfully dons a black wig, accepting a life in which identities may so easily be changed. In the film's last scene, when Claudia is herself replaced by a common whore, she has no moral force left from which to condemn the fickle Sandro. Now totally sophisticated, she can only join him in a gesture of resignation at their common incapacity for commitment.

The plot, or aborted action, of *L'Avventura* advances by means of visual analogies and small appearances; Antonioni can spend seconds shooting Claudia as she sits exhaustedly in the train station where she hopes to escape Sandro's tempting importunities. Above her head, in this actionless scene, are some pictures of madonnas. The moment's meaning is a contrast between the despair registered on Claudia's face and the serenity in the pictures. This is how Antonioni's decor interacts with and interprets the characters.

It also helps to establish the significance of their behavior through visual symbols and allusions, like the modernist devices of *The Waste Land* or *The Magic Mountain,* that realize Antonioni's modernist themes: lovelessness, paralysis of will, loss of faith. Fundamentally, *L'Avventura* contains an implied parallel with the *Odyssey,* which mostly took place in the same Sicilian locale, and which provides the Western mind with its definitive image of adventure and search. The point of the comparison, of course, is that the modern quest, indifferent to its object, must turn inward. Thus Antonioni fills the background with symbols of former validity to point up their debasement in the modern world. I will cite only a few examples. Patrizia, the yacht's owner, works a jigsaw puzzle of a classic scene while the playboy Raimondo fondles her breast in a gesture that is "unreproved, if undesired." On the island, while searching for Anna, the modern Romans find an ancient amphora, and after some humorously uncomprehending guesses about its possible function, Raimondo carelessly lets it fall. The *carabinieri* to whom Sandro goes at Messina are housed in a baroque palace before whose splendid marble walls they have set up ugly wooden slabs to form an office.

Throughout the island sequence, Antonioni is careful to train his cameras on the rocks so that the humans are always seen entering large barren areas, as if they come too late and too punily to dominate the alien landscape. For their humanity has been wrecked by a cultural debacle in which, as in much modern literature, a debilitated pursuit of pleasure competes with activities that had traditionally nurtured the soul. This theme, which gives the meager events their large significance, permeates the film. On the church tower at Noto, for example, when Sandro asks Claudia to marry him, she refuses a proposal so lightly made by ringing the bells which actualize attunement. The Sicilian men milling about Claudia with sidewise lust are visually counterpointed by the choir-boys marching in orderly sexlessness from the cathedral. The Sicilian journey progresses through a culture in ruins (symbolized by the succession of church towers progressively abandoned and incomplete—one without a bell), coming to rest at Taormina, haunt of the rich, before a shattered building of which all that remains is a ruined tower and a fragment of façade.

Because *L'Avventura* shows an unformed girl realizing her latent sophistication, it comes closer than any of Antonioni's films to presenting a character in transition. Although we know little about Claudia (except that she was born poor), we can sympathize with her decline. Thus *L'Avventura*, Antonioniesque though it be, is moving in a conventional way. The later films are more representational in their enactment of cultural malaise, their characters are more fully symbolic, and their effect is more sensory and intellectual.

In *L'Avventura*, although hints exist only to demonstrate the deterioration that is modern worldliness, we learn something not only of Claudia's but of Sandro's past. Once a creator of buildings, Sandro now merely measures their cost. When he vindictively spills ink on the young boy's sketch of the cathedral at Noto, the personal and public meanings of Sandro's behavior merge; he is both a success reacting against lost innocence and modern man reacting against lost faith. In *La Notte,* we do not know why Giovanni can no longer write; the personal drama now merely illustrates the public meaning of a day that begins with the death of an intellectual and ends at an industrialist's party. Similarly, we do not know why Giovanni and Lydia have fallen out of love. Their unhappiness is not explained; it is merely displayed.

To establish Lydia's feelings, for example, Antonioni shoots the famous walking scene in which Lydia's state of mind is revealed through her reactions to a postman eating a sandwich, some fighting youths, a man firing off rockets, *et cetera*. Stopped clocks and flaking walls suggest the era's sickness; later, at the party, Antonioni achieves one of his best visual symbols of deterioration by showing the industrialist's cat staring fixedly at a Roman portrait bust. "Maybe he's waiting for him to wake up," the millionaire's wife announces. "Try and figure cats out." When Giovanni takes Lydia to a night club, they witness the erotic dance of two splendid Negroes; but the act turns out to be acrobatic, concluding when the female manages to get her legs around a glass of water. Milan's sterility is highlighted at the party which becomes vital only when a rainstorm strikes.

With a few exceptions (the explicit last scene or some excessive business at the party), *La Notte* dramatizes its insights subtly. But the film is impure. As if frightened by its increased abstractness, Antonioni relies too heavily on dialogue to clarify his points; and, as we might expect from an artist who thinks with his eyes, the dialogue is banal.

Eclipse is more abstract than *La Notte,* heightening its emphasis on meaningful gesture and replacing dialogue, as often as possible, with expressive natural sound. Vittoria, the heroine, is even less explained than Giovanni and Lydia. We never learn why she has broken off her first affair or why she takes up with Piero. Although she has a job, it is minimally emblematic, whereas the jobs of Sandro and Giovanni represent obvious spiritual problems. Vittoria is created almost exclusively through what she does. She constantly fusses with flowers or disports herself with the primitive and the natural. These meanings come together when Vittoria is fascinated by one of the men who is wiped out by the stock market slide. Whereas the other investors sweat and fan themselves furiously, rush around, or, like Vittoria's mother, blasphemously turn religion to the service of Mammon, this man exits calmly. Vittoria follows him to a café, where he orders a drink and writes intently on a piece of paper. When he leaves, dropping the paper behind him, she retrieves it. It is covered with flowers. She is delighted. This is the moment before she begins her affair with Piero.

Living in a sterile modern world, Vittoria seeks escape on an airplane ride above the clouds, as well as through love. When down to earth in Piero's arms, however, she learns that people nowadays care only for things. The liveliest, noisiest scenes in *Eclipse* take place at the stock exchange (significantly, built in the ruins of a Roman temple), where men sweatingly pursue goods that truly excite them. But, try as they may to stir it, the air cannot cool their agitated bodies. Only above the clouds, or in one small moment when the Exchange halts out of respect for a deceased broker, does the air quicken; during that unique respite from noise in the ruined temple, a large overhead fan, like a propeller, whirs freely.

Setting aside *Red Desert* for the moment, this brief survey of Antonioni's films should suggest the atmosphere of *Blow-Up.* Yet faced with a murder witnessed by a photographer, Bosley Crowther inevitably recalled the Hitchcock of *Rear Window,* and this utterly misleading comparison has been perpetuated by many critics. In fact, the antiplot of *Blow-Up* is *vero Antonioni.*[1]

[1] The Julio Cortázar short story on which *Blow-Up* is loosely based considers a question only hinted at in the film: does art have metaphysical and moral power over reality? Cortázar's hero is an amateur photographer but a professional translator and the first part of his story is a characteristic dissertation on the difficulty of representing life in words.

The main event is the hero's encounter with a young boy and an older, blond woman in the square of an island in the Seine. Thinking he witnesses an act of sexual initiation, he takes a photograph. But when the woman asks that it be

Like *L'Avventura, Blow-Up* concerns the search for something that is never found. As in *La Notte*, the peripatetic hero fails to accomplish anything. Like the other protagonists, the photographer is the embodiment of a role, although here he is so fully defined by his function that he is not even named. As in Antonioni's other films, the climax is reached when the protagonist comes to face his own impotence. There is even a concluding disappearance that recalls the absence of Vittoria and Piero from the last minutes of *Eclipse*: as the camera slowly draws away from the photographer, he slowly diminishes in size, an effect made more significant when Antonioni literally causes him to vanish before "the end."

The events in *Blow-Up* dramatize the same theme one finds in Antonioni's other films. The photographer, a creature of work and pleasure but of no inner force or loyalty, is unable to involve himself in life. He watches it, manipulates it; but, like all of Antonioni's male characters, he has no sense of life's purpose. Thus, when faced with a challenge, he cannot decisively act. Unable to transcend himself, except through ultimate confrontation with his soul, he represents modern paralysis.

Most reviewers have denied that this or any other theme is apparent in *Blow-Up*, while those few who believed that Antonioni was up to something were either uncertain or wrong, I think, about what it was. Since Antonioni demands closer attention than even professional film watchers are likely to be familiar with, and since reviewers usually have the sketchiest knowledge of a serious director's canon, the errors are not surprising. But what are we to make of the critical misconceptions perpetrated by John Simon?

---

returned, an older man, who had been watching the scene from a car, interrupts their altercation. During the argument, the boy escapes, convincing the translator that, despite his meddling, "taking the photo had been a good act." When he returns home and blows up the photograph, however, he concludes that the older woman was apparently seducing the boy for the man. Revolted by what he has witnessed, the photographer now imaginatively relives the experience, trying to release the boy from the imagined horror just as he had released him from the actual scene.

Antonioni's transformations are nearly total: the ages of the couple are reversed, she becomes dark-haired, the scene takes place in a garden rather than a square, seduction becomes murder. More important, the art theme is made peripheral (by introducing a literal artist as a foil to the commercial, mechanical photographer), while Antonioni focuses on the social context that he invents for the episode. I can think of no better way to illustrate the profoundly social orientation of Antonioni.

Notice, too, that whereas Cortázar's hero never discovers whether his "good act" was really effectual, Antonioni's photographer learns that he accomplished nothing. Cortázar's territory is the imagination, where fabulous victories match equally fabulous defeats; Antonioni's world is sadly, unconquerably real.

Simon is, in my opinion, the best American film critic now writing. Expectedly, he was the one critic who saw the need to summarize *Blow-Up*'s events; yet in his exhaustive resumé, he missed the crucial moments. As a result, he determined that Antonioni's theme was Pirandellian, despite the total absence of any metaphysical concern in the director's other work. Together with a common emphasis on Hitchcock, this Pirandellian analogy has done a great deal to obfuscate Antonioni's meaning.

Because the body vanishes, and because the photographer ultimately hears a tennis ball that doesn't exist, some people have thought that Antonioni means us to question the existence of the corpse. Incidental details such as the photographer's initial appearance as a bum who surprisingly enters a Rolls Royce have been cited in support of this interpretation. Yet the point of the first scene is that the photographer *isn't* a bum, that he took part in the doss-house life merely to exploit it for his picture book. The body exists; what is significant is that the photographer didn't realize he'd seen it.

When the narrator enters the park, we see him performing his first spontaneous gesture. Emerging from the antique shop, he notices it and, for no apparent reason, enters. Perhaps he is attracted by the lush greenness, the melodically rustling leaves. Chancing on the love ballet, however, the photographer responds automatically, according to a settled routine. Love, as his agent, Ron, later tells him, would make a "truer" conclusion to his picture book. But when the girl tries to get his film and a young man (apparently the murderer) peers through the restaurant window at his lunch with Ron, the photographer begins to suspect that he has witnessed something less than innocent. After the girl leaves his studio, he blows up the photographs; and it is here, I think, that Simon and every other critic I have read misinterpret the action.

What happens is this: While the photographer is studying the shots, he spies something suspicious in the still of some shrubbery behind a fence. What he does not see but what the audience does, as Antonioni's lens pans across the row of blowups, is the still showing a body. The audience, but not the photographer, knows that a body exists. (When Vanessa Redgrave ran away from the photographer during the park scene, she stopped to look down at the tree, from behind which a head was unmistakably visible.) But the photographer chooses to blow up only the still showing the murderer and his gun. Exulting in what he thinks is a meaningful action, he rushes to the phone to call his agent. "Somebody was trying to kill somebody else," he says, "I saved his life."

That the photographer jumps to this erroneous conclusion despite contrary evidence is logical in view of subtle but clear hints we got earlier of a latent dissatisfaction with his normal mode of behavior. His studio is dominated by photographs of a sky diver and a skin diver, his living room by a shot of camels (recalling a similar photograph in *Eclipse*), and he clearly would like to get away. Vittoria made her frail gesture in a plane; the photographer buys a propeller. Lydia had gone on a solitary walk; the photographer, so far as he knows, takes a stroll in the park. As he tells his agent, "I've gone off London this week. Doesn't do anything for me. I'm fed up with those bloody bitches. Wish I had tons of money, then I'd be free."

Freedom and mastery are cheaply purchased when the photographer allows himself to believe he has saved a man's life. Had he done so, his action would have symbolized a separation from the aimless mod world. What he witnessed, as he believes, was the attempt by a young swinger to murder a gray-haired, older man in a garden. Catching the snake hidden in the bushes, the photographer had preserved the intended victim. The fact of the matter is different. . . . Hiding behind a tree, like the murderer, he shot with a camera what the latter shot with a gun; and he did not save the older man. He is blond, and so is the murderer. For all his aloof contempt, he is as frivolous as the mod clowns who frame his experience. In the last scene, when he hears their "tennis ball," he effectively actualizes the charade existence that they share in common. His final gesture of resignation—like Sandro's tears, Giovanni's loveless copulation, or Piero's and Vittoria's failure to meet—shows clearly that the photographer cannot change.

The actions I have sketched are nearly pantomimed; their larger implications are also established through visual means. As with the *carabinieri*'s office in *L'Avventura*, the first shot in *La Notte* (showing a graceful old building standing in front of Pirelli's glass box), the forbidding sleekness of E.U.R. in *Eclipse*, Antonioni fills the background in *Blow-Up* with examples of tradition being razed to make way for a gray, anonymous wasteland. As the photographer drives through London, the camera pans along the colorful walls of the old city only to be abruptly lost in blank space surrounding a new housing project—all grays and browns. When he visits the antique shop, scouting real estate for his agent, he advises purchase since the neighborhood seems to have attracted homosexuals—those great contemporary buyers of the past. The old caretaker, however, refuses to sell him anything, but the young mod owner is only too anxious to turn the shop into cash for a trip to Nepal, where she hopes to escape from the antiques. "Nepal is all antiques," the photographer dryly observes.

The modern world, however, seems bent on destroying its traditions. On the wall of the photographer's apartment, an old Roman tablet is overwhelmed by the hallucinatory violence of the modern painting at its side. More important, traditional human pursuits are being drained of their force. Politics is now playacting; a pacifist parade marches by with signs bearing inscriptions like "No," or "On. On. On." or "Go away." Pleasure is narcotizing, whether at the "pot" party or in the rock 'n roll club. Love is unabsorbing, as the photographer learns from his friend's marriage. Art has lost its validity. Murder is ignored.

These last implications are forcefully portrayed in the film's main scenes of human interaction. The first of these scenes shows the photographer visiting his friend Bill, who is a painter. When the hero enters his flat, the painter is standing affectedly before a large canvas. Attempting to engage the photographer's interest, he explains his condition:

> They don't mean anything when I do them, just a mess. Afterward, I find something to hang onto [pointing]—like that leg. Then it all sorts itself out; it's like finding a clue in a detective story.

Although we are likely to find Bill rather pretentious, particularly in view of the obviously derivative nature of his painting, the photographer seems unusually impressed. When the painter's wife enters, he tells her that he has wanted to buy one of the canvases. When we see her massaging his neck with obvious interest on her part but mere friendly comfort on his, we know what this oasis of art and domesticity might mean to a man so cynical and frenetic. Later, in his puzzlement concerning the murder, when he turns to them for help, he discovers that the oasis is dry.

In the second important scene, the murderer's accomplice meets the photographer at his studio because he blew his car horn when he reached his street so as to inform the pursuers of his whereabouts. When he tries to calm her, she replies:

> "My private life is already in a mess. It would be a disaster—"
> P: "So what? Nothing like a little disaster for sorting things out."

Through turning sparse, functional dialogue into a system of verbal echoes, Antonioni achieves the economy of tight verse. Yet he does not sacrifice naturalness. The painter, in an observation appropriate to the scene, had suggested that visual experience is comprehensible only through recollection, during which process it performs the function of a clue that helps to "sort things out." The photographer, in a casual remark to the girl, asserts that the sorting out process is facilitated by disaster. This verbal cross-reference points to the meaning behind the action.

The most subtle use of dialogue occurs in a sequence which has been either ignored or misinterpreted as a sign that Antonioni's theme is failure of communication. When the painter's wife enters his studio, she comes upon a distraught man; he has lost his evidence and his faith in his friends. Although laconically, they do communicate:

P: "Do you ever think of leaving [your husband]?"
W: "No, I don't think so."
P: [Turning away with annoyance] "I saw a man killed this morning."
W: "Where? Was he shot?"
P: "Sort of a park."
W: "Are you sure?"
P: "He's still there."
W: "Who was he?"
P: "Someone."
W: "How did it happen?"
P: "I don't know. I didn't see."
W: [Bewildered] "You didn't see?"
P: [Wry grimace] "No."
W: "Shouldn't you call the police?"
P: [Pointing to the one still the murderer didn't take] "That's the body."
W: "Looks like one of Bill's paintings. [Turning to him, helplessly] Will you help me? I don't know what to do. [He doesn't react. She looks at the shot.] What is it? Hmmmm. I wonder why they shot him."
P: "I didn't ask."
W: [Looks up at him, smiles sadly, and, after some hesitation, leaves.]

I record this dialogue to show how clearly and economically Antonioni establishes his meaning.[2] When the painter's wife comes to his

[2] The dialogue at the "pot" party is equally clear. After great difficulty, the photographer succeeds in getting Ron to listen to his problem:

P: "Somone's been killed."
R: "O.K."
P: "Listen, those pictures I took in the park—[No response] I want you to see the corpse. We've got to get a shot of it."
R: [Bewildered] "I'm not a photographer."
P: [Bitterly] "I am."
R: [Nonplussed] "What did you see in that park?"
P: [Resignedly] "Nothing." [Ron, who can't focus his eyes well, motions the

apartment, she hears the photographer's confession of failure and declares her own Bill's art is no alternative to the destruction symbolized by the murder; his art is another version of it. They can no more deal with their marriage than the photographer can deal with the crime. She can only slink away in compassion for their mutual impotence, leaving him to futile pursuit, marijuana, and his depressing moment of truth.

In *Blow-Up*, as in *Eclipse* and *L'Avventura*'s island sequence, Antonioni achieves his meanings through the use of sound effects as well as speech. When the photographer shoots his model in a parody of intercourse, and when he poses the mannequins, music, as he says, is "noise" to inspire their artificial vitality. When Vanessa Redgrave comes to his apartment, fresh from the murder, he tries to teach her the lesson that music maintains one's "cool." While giving her some "pot," to which she sensuously yields herself, he shows her that really to enjoy it and the taped jazz he is playing, she must hold herself back —draw slowly and keep time against the beat. Before he begins to inspect the blowups, he turns the jazz on. But the music quickly fades when he becomes involved; as he looks deeply into the frames, we hear on the sound track a rustling of leaves.

The incredible greenness of a park that was the ironic setting for murder suggests another of Antonioni's means. When the photographer discovers the body's loss, he looks up at the tree, whose leaves now rattle angrily, and sees the leaves as black against a white sky. Like the sound analogies and the verbal cross-references, the color in *Blow-Up* aids comprehension.

The film is composed mainly in four hues: black, white, green and purple. The hero's studio is black and white, as are most of his clothes and those of Vanessa Redgrave. So too are photographs. In fact, the meaning of the event in the park was "as clear as black and white" before he photographed it, which is what makes for significance in his initial failure of perception as well as in his underlying failure to understand the implication of his way of life. The green park was penetrated by evil. Suitably, the door of the photographer's dark room, in which he brings to light the dark deed, is also green. Not, however, until he copulates with the teenyboppers in a sea of purple does he realize that he did not prevent the crime. Appropriately, the door to the room in which he blows up the fatal still is also purple. One of the teenyboppers wears purple tights; the other, green.

---

photographer to follow him. The photographer does. Next scene shows him waking up from the debauch.]

Colorful though it is, *Blow-Up* seems to be moving toward colorless-ness, black and white—almost as if Antonioni were trying to make us face the skull beneath the painted flesh. But that is not what most re-viewers have done. That they should, if my reading is correct, have missed the film's meaning so completely is a phenomenon almost as significant as the film itself. What, after all, does their error tell us?

The familiar things are aspects of a fixed condition. As I have said, few reviewers know the director's work; fewer still have sophisticated ideas about film art. Their collective sophistication, if not their in-telligence, is modest; when they simulate brilliance, it is only through the perfervid prose we associate with *Time* magazine. I doubt that many serious readers would choose books on the advice of the same sources to which, *faute de mieux*, they are forced to turn for evaluation of films. This much, I think, is sadly inarguable, but not limited to consideration of *avant-garde* film-making in general or Antonioni in particular.

The confusion about Antonioni comes from the unusual demands he makes. Most films are to be looked at; Antonioni's are to be in-spected. Decades of film as a commercial form of escapism have atro-phied our perception; like all great artists, Antonioni insists that we see anew. Unfortunately, most reviewers can't see. Although many dis-guised their ineptitude by reporting little of what goes on in *Blow-Up*, distressing errors of fact tend to characterize the more venturesome accounts. Thus one reviewer (Richard Corliss, *National Review*) has the photographer buying an oar, while another (Joseph Morgenstern, *Newsweek*) has the orgy spread out on sky-blue paper. John Simon suggests that the photographer makes eyes at Sarah Miles, whereas the reverse is true. As a result of this error, he can give no accurate reading of the subplot. John Coleman (*New Statesman*) loftily deems *Blow-Up* a "very superficial film . . . about people reckoned as leading super-ficial lives"; but since he asserts that the photographer saw the body and the gun *after* the orgy sequence, Coleman is in no position to call anyone superficial.

Such errors of fact are less important in themselves than as manifesta-tions of a cavalier attitude toward Antonioni's difficult style. More than their mistakes, the arrogance of reviewers is what rankles. Confronted with a famously complex director whose films are widely acknowledged to be important, the journeyman critic, both here and in England, treats *Blow-Up* as if it were indeed a mechanical piece of Hitchcock. Despite museum cults, the emergence of cinema's right to be considered a form of art is notoriously recent. A parallel growth in movie review-ing is long overdue.

Among critics, the source of confusion is more profound. Misunderstanding *Blow-Up* is not only failure to scrutinize with sufficient care a highly wrought method of expression; it is the consequence of some false, but currently powerful, ideas about the nature of art. Although these ideas are more blatantly damaging with an art form so ill-defined as cinema, they have their origin in wider cultural presuppositions.

The first of them, to use Norman Podhoretz's phrase, is the demand that art "bring the news." Widespread dissatisfaction with contemporary fiction, lack of interest in poetry, and the inflation of nonfictional forms like the book review all indicate the dominance of this aesthetic program. Thus Norman Mailer's lucubrations attain significance because he styles himself a social prophet, confessional poetry becomes the accepted fashion in verse, and nonfiction, a form defined by what it isn't, now begins to absorb whatever it lacks.

From the neonaturalist perspective, *Blow-Up* is offensive because it manipulates the materials of contemporary London to express not the city but Antonioni's version of modern life. If one can bear the hip language—not unrelated to the ideas—he can see this attitude clearly expressed in Richard Goldstein's article in the *Village Voice,* entitled "The Screw-Up." Condemning a lack of "understanding that can only be called Parental," Goldstein insists that Antonioni misrepresents the swinging Samarkand and derides the film for the expressiveness that—*autres temps, autres moeurs*—would have guaranteed its status as a work of art. Whatever can be said for such documentary emphasis, it easily degenerates into mindless fixation on the up-to-date. That people old enough to know better don't avoid the trap can be seen in Pauline Kael's review, where, amidst a veritable fusillade, she criticizes Antonioni for not catching "the humor and fervor and astonishing speed in youth's rejection of older values." Godard, *si!* Antonioni, *no!*

The other new aesthetic barbarism has quickly filtered down to its rightful level, having been recently promoted . . . by the arts editor of *Look.* Given a more respectable formulation by Susan Sontag, Richard Gilman and other less conspicuous gurus, the conception of art as "sensuous form" might seem a useful antidote to excess verisimilitude, but it comes to much the same thing. Like those who wish art to be a form of sociology, the advocates of a "new sensibility" reveal a fatal affinity for what's "in." Thus Miss Sontag finds that formal heights are scaled by happenings, pornography and science fiction, while critics like Gilman opt for novels (promoted by magazines like the *New Yorker*) in which insouciance becomes art by imitating the era's bafflement.

. . . One error encourages the sentimental social pieties of some

reviewers; the other authorizes their imperception. Thus reviews of
Blow-Up express outraged social optimism or a kind of aesthetic trance
induced by globules of "surface beauty." The skillful creation of symbols for insight—art, in short—becomes an achievement of negligible
appeal.

A third aesthetic error (born, in part, out of reaction against the
other two), despite a devotion to artistic seriousness, runs the risk of
blocking new modes. John Simon is rightly opposed to art without dis-
cursive implications or rational validity. In *Hudson Review* pieces
concerning Albee, Pinter, and thinkers like McLuhan and N. O.
Brown, Simon shows himself a powerful demolition machine for a
culture beseiged on all sides. But in his splendid assaults, he sometimes
finds himself forced backward into old-fashioned demands for situa-
tional realism, psychologically valid motivation, and humanistically
oriented themes. These requirements should be suspended with considerably less alacrity than most critics now show, but they must be
abandoned for those rare cases, like Borges, Beckett or Antonioni, in
which authentic art is being produced in a new way. Significantly,
Simon is receptive to such art when reviewing books—a further indication that people automatically relax their aesthetics when discussing
films.

A similarly based lack of sympathy is detectable in the otherwise
laudatory pieces on Antonioni's earlier films that Dwight Macdonald
wrote for *Esquire*. Although Macdonald, along with Stanley Kauffmann, was one of Antonioni's few discerning American champions, he
became displeased by the Italian's progressive refusal to motivate his
characters. Even Kauffmann was made nervous by the abstractionism
of *Eclipse*, although he rejoiced, wrongly as I think, in the colored
abstractionism of *Red Desert*.

Still, despite a few hints of retrograde commitment, Simon, Kauffmann and Macdonald are the most sensitive of Antonioni's American
critics and the most useful, intelligent film critics of recent times. The
fumbling responses of their colleagues remind us that the always thinly
staffed legion of competence is now threatened either with depopulation
or, as was seen when Wilfrid Sheed replaced Dwight Macdonald at
Esquire and Pauline Kael took over Stanley Kauffmann's post at *The
New Republic,* with specious new recruits.

As a novelist and book or theater critic, Wilfrid Sheed has behind
him an estimable body of work. As a film critic, he has nothing—either
in experience or rumination—a fact that he candidly admitted in his
first *Esquire* piece. Despite his avowed respect for Antonioni's other
films, his review of *Blow-Up* expresses nearly ruthless contempt. Much
of the piece is not about the film at all, concentrating its attention in-

stead (complete with feeble jokes about old musicals that Sheed *does* know) on Rex Reed's interview with Antonioni in the *Times*. The rest of his review repeats Judith Crist's complaint that Antonioni let a good story get away, Richard Goldstein's complaint that Antonioni didn't really capture London, and the blank raving about "surface beauty" that characterizes most other reviews. Finding the symbolism "non-organic" and the ideas banal, Sheed disdains to argue either point.

Such offenses against criticism are compounded in Miss Kael's review by offenses against taste, logic and the reader's patience. In a piece so staggeringly verbose that one cannot, as in Sheed's case, attribute the lack of argument to lack of space, Miss Kael serves up that combination of personal exhibitionism, obsession with fashion, and irrelevant inside dope that has become her special ragout. She reviews not the film but the audience.

Will *Blow-Up* be taken seriously in 1968 only by the same sort of cultural die-hards who are still sending out five-page single-spaced letters on their interpretation of *Marienbad?* (No two are alike, no one interesting.) It has some of the *Marienbad* appeal: a friend phones for your opinion and when you tell him you didn't much care for it, he says, "You'd better see it again, I was at a swinging party the other night and it's all anybody ever talked about!" (Was there ever a good movie that everybody was talking about?) It probably won't blow over because it also has the *Morgan!-Georgy Girl* appeal; people identify with it so strongly, they get *upset* if you don't like it—as if you were rejecting not just the movie but *them*. And in a way they're right, because if you don't accept the peculiarly slugged consciousness of *Blow-Up,* you *are* rejecting something in them. Antonioni's new mixture of suspense with vagueness and confusion seems to have the kind of numbing fascination for them that they associate with art and intellectuality, and they are responding to it as *their* film—and hence as a masterpiece.

Two bad reviews by two irresponsible critics prove little; but when we search for alternatives, the point gets made. There are frequently fewer interesting plays or books in a given season than interesting films. Yet I think the *Blow-Up* controversy suggests how ill-equipped American criticism is to discuss them. With the exceptions of John Simon and Stanley Kauffmann, who recently returned to *The New Republic,* there are at the moment, no aesthetically sophisticated and informed guides available for the growing audience that seeks enlightenment about films. . . . Of the journalistic film reviewers, there is scarcely one to be taken seriously. The mass magazines used to employ men like

Agee or Macdonald, but such critics have been ill-replaced. Smaller film quarterlies (when they last long enough to be useful) are made up either by film buffs capable, like the *Cahiers du Cinéma* crowd, of ontological analyses of Jerry Lewis, or they bear the same relationship to live film criticism that a philological journal bears to the vital discussion of books.

Artists like Antonioni will continue to progress, unperturbed by widespread ignorance. (Moreover, they will prosper; *Variety* says *Blow-Up* is "k.o.") But scores of interested viewers will be left behind.

REVIEWS

No Antoniennui

by ANDREW SARRIS

Michelangelo Antonioni's *Blow-Up* (at the Coronet) is the movie of the year, and I use the term "movie" advisedly for an evening's entertainment that left me feeling no pain (or Antoniennui) whatsoever. It is possible that this year's contributions from Ford, Dreyer, Hitchcock, Chabrol, and Godard may cut deeper and live longer than Antonioni's mod masterpiece, but no other movie this year has done as much to preserve my faith in the future of the medium. If you have not yet seen *Blow-Up*, see it immediately before you hear or read anything more about it. I speak from personal experience when I say it is better to let the movie catch you completely unawares. One of its greatest virtues is surprise, and the last thing you want is to know the plot and theme in advance. Unfortunately, most of the reviewers have given the show completely away. Judith Crist coyly conceals the plot gambit in *Gambit,* but she spills the beans on *Blow-Up* with no qualms whatsoever. Why? I suppose she considers *Blow-Up* too esoteric for audiences to enjoy in the course of mindless moviegoing. It's a pity since, purely on a plot level, *Blow-Up* provides more thrills, chills, and fancy frissons than any other movie this year.

The excitement begins with the opening credits which are stenciled across a field of green grass opening into a pop blue rhythm and blues background of dancing models perceived only partially through the lettering which, among other things, implicates Antonioni in the script and heralds Vanessa Redgrave, David Hemmings, Sarah Miles, and a supporting cast of unknowns. The billing is misleading. Miss Redgrave and Miss Miles make only guest appearances in what amounts to a vehicle for David Hemmings and Antonioni's camera. *Blow-Up* is never dramatically effective in terms of any meaningful confronta-

From The Village Voice, *December 29, 1966, p. 19. Copyright* © *1970 by* The Village Voice. *Reprinted by permission of* The Village Voice.

tions of character. The dialogue is self-consciously spare and elliptical in a sub-Pinteresque style. Fortunately, the 24-hour duration of the plot makes it possible for Antonioni to disguise most of the film as a day in the life of a mod photographer in swinging London town. What conflict there is in *Blow-Up* is captured in the opening clash between vernal greens on one plane and venal blues, reds, yellows, pinks, and purples on another. The natural world is arrayed against the artificial scene; conscience is deployed against convention.

The film itself begins with more obvious contrasts. A lorry loaded with screaming revelers made up in garishly painted mime faces. Cut to derelicts trudging silently out of flophouse with bundles and belongings. One would suspect Antonioni of facile Marxist montage in his cross-cutting between mimes and derelicts, between noisy merriment and quiet morning afterment, but one would be wrong. The mimes are merely an Italianate mannerism in London, and the derelicts are simply the grubbier side of a photographer's visual concerns. Nevertheless, the cross-cutting functions by itself without any explicatory dialogue or commentary. Even the protagonist is identified for us only by degrees. Antonioni can afford a leisurely exposition for two reasons. First, we are going to be looking at Hemmings all through the movie, and a slightly mysterious materialization will not hurt him at the outset. Secondly, the emphasis throughout is not so much on the protagonist himself as on what he and his camera see and on how well he blends in with the background. Gradually we are filled in not so much with a plot as with a routine—a day in the life of a candid cameraman.

Blow-Up abounds with what Truffaut calls "privileged moments," intervals of beautiful imagery while nothing seems to be happening to develop the drama or advance the narrative. Very early in the film, the camera confronts the photographer's long black convertible head-on at a crossroads. Suddenly the entire screen is blotted out by a blue bus streaking across from right to left, followed by a yellow truck. That sudden splash of blue and yellow defines Antonioni's mood and milieu better than any set of speeches ever could. Wherever Antonioni's camera goes, doors, fences, poles, even entire buildings seem to have been freshly painted for the sake of chromatic contrast or consistency. Part of Antonioni's ambivalence toward his subject in *Blow-Up* is reflected in the conflicting temptations of documentary and decoration. After painting the trees in *The Red Desert* a petrified gray, Antonioni feels no compunctions about painting an outdoor phone booth in *Blow-Up* a firehouse red. If reality is not expressive enough, a paint brush will take up the slack. This theory of controlled color is carried about as far as it can go in *Blow-Up* before its artistic limitations become too apparent. Antonioni is heading in a dangerous direction, but the

Pirandellian resolution of the plot saves him on this occasion from the stylistically bloated decadence of *The Red Desert*.

The ultimate beauty of *Blow-Up* is derived from the artistic self-revelation of the director. *Blow-Up* is to Antonioni what *Lola Montes* was to the late Max Ophuls, what *Ugetsu* was to the late Kenji Mizoguchi, what *Contempt* was to Godard, what *French Can-Can* was to Renoir, what *Limelight* was to Chaplin, what *Rear Window* was to Hitchcock, what *8½* was to Fellini—a statement of the artist not on life, but on art itself as the consuming passion of an artist's life. As David Hemmings moves gracefully through off-beat sites in London, his body writhing to meet the challenge of every new subject, we feel that Antonioni himself is intoxicated by the sensuous surfaces of a world he wishes to satirize. Curiously, he is more satisfying when he succumbs to the sensuousness than when he stands outside it. The unsuccessful sequences—the rock 'n' roll session, the marijuana party, the alienation conversations between Hemmings and Vanessa Redgrave in one scene and Sarah Miles in another—all suffer from the remoteness of cold chronicles recorded by an outsider. Antonioni is more successful when he forgets his ennui long enough to photograph a magnificent mod fashion spectacle which transcends the grotesquely artificial creatures that lend themselves to the illusion. Even more spectacular is the teeny bopper sandwich orgy which digresses from the main plot. An entire generation of mini-teasers and inhibited exhibitionists are divested of their defenses in a frenzied choreography of bold beauty and heart-rending contemporaneity. The stripping away of pink and blue leotards may explain why the Metro lion has decided to skulk away from the opening credits like a timid pussy cat scared of the Production Code.

The fact that Antonioni can be entertaining even when he is not enlightening makes the eruption of his plot all the more stunning. It starts simmering in the midst of apparent aimlessness. The photographer-protagonist wanders out of an antique shop, drifts by chance into a park where he ignores a grotesquely sexless park attendant jabbing trash with her pike, passes by a tennis court where two children are playing a clumsy brand of tennis, photographs pigeons afoot and in flight, then stalks a pair of lovers up a hill. At a distance, it looks like a tall girl pulling at an older man in what later will be recalled in retrospect as a spectacle of carnal Calvary [Plate VII]. Here Hemmings becomes a weak-kneed voyeur as he scurries behind fences and trees with his telescopic lens. This is raw, spontaneous Life in an ominously leafy setting. Vanessa Redgrave, she of the incredibly distracting long legs and elongated spinal column extended vertically through an ugly blue-plaid mini-suit making her look at a distance like a seven-foot

girl guide, in short, Vanessa Redgrave via Antonioni rather than Karel
(*Morgan!*) Reisz, runs up to Hemmings to plead for the pictures, but
everything in the movie has been so fragmented up to this time that we
accept her trivial invasion of privacy argument at face value. Hemmings refuses to return the negatives, and later tricks her into accepting bogus negatives while he develops and "blows up" the real ones.
What seemed like a tryst in a park is magnified into a murder. Death
which has hovered over Antonioni's films from the very beginning of
his career makes its grand entrance in a photographer's studio through
the eyes of a camera which sees truth whereas the eyes of the photographer see only reality. This then is the paradox of Antonioni's vision of
art: The further we draw away from reality, the closer we get to the
truth. Vanessa Redgrave, an irritating, affected personality in her
"live" scenes, comes to life with a vengeance in the "blow-up" of her
photos.

From the moment of his artistic triumph, the protagonist becomes
morally impotent. He has discovered truth, but is unable to pass judgment or secure justice. He returns to the scene of the crime that night
and finds the corpse of the murdered man. He visits a neighboring
artist and mistress only to find them furiously flagrante delicto. He
returns to his studio and discovers the theft of his blow-ups. He is
physically frightened when he hears footsteps and begins to cower in a
corner of his decor. It is only the artist's mistress (Sarah Miles) treading
as beautifully as ever on her cat feet and in her transparent dress. He
tells her about the murder, but she is too preoccupied with her own
problems to give him much help. The rest of the film threatens to degenerate into one of Antonioni's shaggy dog Odysseys to futility when
the photographer returns to the scene of the blown-up crime. The
wind is blowing. The body is gone. The leaves flutter with chilling indifference. Then suddenly the mime revelers from the opening sequence reappear in their loaded lorry and disembark at the tennis
court. Two mimes play an imaginary game with somewhat clumsy gestures while the others watch with silent, swivel-headed concentration.
Antonioni's camera begins following the action of the imaginary ball
back and forth across the net until it is "hit" over the fence near where
the photographer is standing. He walks back to the spot where the
"ball" has landed, and throws it back. He then begins swiveling his
head back and forth, and even hears the ball bouncing. He smiles at
his own susceptibility, but suddenly an expression of pain flashes across
his face. The camera cuts to an overhead shot of the photographer, a
self-judgment of both contempt and compassion. Antonioni, the ex-
tennis player who once sold his trophies to live, has come out in the
open with a definitive description of his divided sensibility, half Mod,

half Marxist. Unlike Fellini, however, Antonioni has converted his confession into a genuine movie which objectifies his obsessions without whining or self-pity. As befits the classical tradition of moviemaking, *Blow-Up* can be enjoyed by moviegoers who never heard of Antonioni.

BLOW-UP
by F. A. MACKLIN

Michelangelo Antonioni's *Blow-up* is an important film, but the range of its brilliance gives it the effect of a tour de force. Perhaps it tries to do too much.

Antonioni's world is one of disengagement and sharp contrasts. An early scene has the photographer (David Hemmings) mounting a model as she writhes in disciplined abandon. Striving for the effect, he cries "Yes! Yes! Yes!" as he takes the photographs. This is relative to the "No! No! No!" on the sign of a peace marcher in the street. Both are frozen exclamations, manifestations of passionless intensity. The "Go away" on another peace sign echoes through the film. A young antique shop owner wants to sell her shop to get away from antiques, but she wants to go to Nepal where, the photographer reminds her, "everything is antique." The photographer himself wants to leave London because it no longer does anything for him.

The disengagement is thorough. The propeller that Hemmings finds in the antique shop is perhaps the major symbol of the early part of the film. There is a photograph of a plane in the antique shop, and there is a photograph of a parachutist in Hemming's room. While the latter picture may represent his leap or fall (his abandon in space), the propeller is tangible evidence of the disengagement. Its delivery even halts his progress with the woman (Vanessa Redgrave).

Blow-up is a film in which everything is contradictory, inconsistent, relative to its environment. Antonioni provides a wry social comment when Hemmings flees a rock-music session with a hunk from the smashed guitar of one of the performers (who trampled it himself in frustration) and is chased by an envious mob. When he gets away he tosses the trophy aside; a young man stops to see what it is, then he too drops it.

The film is full of the inconsistencies of talk. Hemmings talks to someone on the phone. He tells the woman the call is for her, then that it is not. Then he says he has been speaking with his wife, then that he is not married. He says they have children, then that they do not. Finally he says the woman on the phone is easy to live with, then he admits that not even this is true.

If disengagement and contradiction are primary elements in *Blow-up* so too are innocence and the inexplicable corruption that accompanies it. *Blow-up* is a film about ignorance and loss—something gone, gone in the way that Hemmings disappears from the green earth at the last flickers of the picture. Something is gone from London, something gone from the antique shop, something gone from the woman's relationship (Sarah Miles) with his neighbor, something gone from the young girls in their modern estrus rollicking naked through the paper—innocence is too easy a term for it. Its loss is replaced by something else, something that keeps things going. Is it imagination? Is it activity: mockery and mime?

The best thing about *Blow-up* is its brilliant metaphor for the creative process: the blow-ups and what they ultimately reveal secreted in the picture. . . . The emphasis upon recognition is beautifully done, and the fact that the photographer's pictures of the park scene are stolen and he is left only with one shot of the corpse blown up from a tiny region of one of the central pictures is fascinating and suggestive of the frustrations and incompleteness of the creative act. There is the inability to communicate it. One can focus, order, express, but the communication depends on others—on the editor who is numbed by drugs at the party. The photographer too becomes disengaged.

The photographer *sees* the corpse (a fact which undermines the theory that overrates the reality-illusion aspect of the film), and he wants someone else to see it. When he returns alone to the park, the day after the party, the corpse is gone. *Blow-up* comes to a natural end at this point with the disappearance of the corpse. That it goes on is Antonioni's decision.

In its concluding emphasis on reality and illusion *Blow-up* is reminiscent of Ingmar Bergman's *The Magician* with its swinging lantern that gives that film a final mirthful gesture. The final scene here is of a mime tennis match between a man and woman in white face, two clowns in a zestful parody. When the imaginary ball goes awry, the photographer returns it—he is brought into being a participant in the phantom action. As he throws the ball the camera remains on him, and then the *sound* of the ball becomes clear. The photographer has been brought into imagination or else he is exiled from it, or both. Is the mime vacant or saving, or both? Like the heartbeat that Julian hears at the end of Edward Albee's *Tiny Alice,* the sound may be real or hallucinatory.

This additional vignette changes the mood and concentration of the film. The clowns (like the tootling band at the end of Fellini's $8\frac{1}{2}$) seem out of another world. It is as though Antonioni has plunged into the world of Fellini (it is a fascinating world, but it is another world), and Antonioni's plunge spends his impact for a different one.

When the photographer tells the editor that he has captured something "peaceful" in his shots in the park, this is not complete. There is shock to be found. This level of illusion has force and scope, but the game at the end substitutes a more common level.

The game was the point to which Antonioni chose to let his film evolve. In sorting it out, this was where he decided to end it. But it ends not tight and complete, but loosening and incomplete—in drama and activity. The latter part seems the foundation of another film (perhaps one already made by another director). Is it necessary to replace the loss of the corpse in this film? Is it necessary or progressive to take those extra steps?

The most memorable scene in *Blow-up* is when the photographer attempts to solve the problems of the photographs he has taken in the park. He becomes aware of the disturbing look on the woman's face, the direction of her glance, the odd stance of the man—it all drips and explodes into meaning. Tedium and inspiration. The confusion, the galling wonder, the discovery, the correlating—step by step a creation evolves before one. Order, and the interpretation of that order, becomes clear. At first he interprets that he has saved a man from death; then he realizes he has witnessed murder.

One wants and needs to savor and contemplate the recognition, the sorting out, the creative act. But clowns rush in and rob the taste, the feeling. Is it right for one to complain because a director gives him too much, far too quickly?

BLOW-UP
by CAREY HARRISON

Unshaven, red-eyed, dressed in rags, a group of men emerge wearily from a slum dosshouse. It is early morning. A young man separates himself from the group, turns down a side street, and climbs into a limousine. He drives to work: his destination proves to be a fashion photographer's studio. Without changing, the young man grabs his camera and plunges into the routine, bobbing and weaving as he photographs the models, barking at them, shouting. The sweat-stained tramp disguise looks bizarre against the antiseptic chic of the sets. It turns out that Thomas is a fashion photographer who hates his work and despises his subjects; he lives for reportage photography, and the dosshouse sequence is to form a central part of his forthcoming book of Cartier Bresson-style photographs. The first mystery of the film is resolved.

With *Blow-Up* Michelangelo Antonioni has turned to making films in English, and while the film was being shot in London last year, speculation was intense. The film was said to be a devastating exposé of the swinging scene and the lascivious world of fashion photography; the movie became a cult among its expected subjects. But *Blow-Up* is not a study in decadence. His easy life cramps the central character's initiative, and contempt for his own success has upset his values: he regards fashion photography and the fashionable world as utterly unreal, documentary photography and the outside world as completely 'real.' The discrimination is too glib, and the shock is all the more severe when he discovers that the outside world is just as opaque as the sets inside his studio. There is no 'more real' world. The affluent life is the context of this discovery, and not the subject of the film's investigation. Perhaps Antonioni saw, too, that 'swinging London' exists only as a trap for amateur sociologists: the biggest common factor among the

Reprinted from Sight and Sound, *37 (Spring 1967): 60–62. Copyright © 1967 by the British Film Institute. Reprinted by permission of the editor.*

'swinging people' is their anxiety to disown all common factors between them and other 'swinging people.' Their membership card is to
have joined no club, which permits each of them to deride the squalid
'scene,' and look forward to *Blow-Up*'s revelations without feeling
exposed.

But Antonioni has not let himself be used. He is not concerned
with the fashion photographer as icon of the pop world, nor with the
idolatry of the girls who surround him. The hero doesn't need them:
he ignores both status and personal relations. As a photographer, he
believes he has a consuming, satisfactory relationship with reality, the
surface of reality, the subject matter of his art. And the crisis he experiences is with his material, not with the women in his life. By means of
the camera he believes himself to be a faithful interpreter of reality,
and when his means prove fallible, all his self-confidence is challenged.
For the first time in his life, it seems, he realises how deceptive reality
can be, that all his life it has been unfaithful to him and his camera.
The audience experiences the film as a series of similar discoveries. The
opening shot presents a group of tramps, but we are already deceived:
one of them is a rich young man in disguise. And like us, Thomas himself is gulled by the properties of the camera, and finally undeceived
by it. In the little deceptions of the film, Antonioni invites us to share
Thomas' downfall as well as observe it.

Thomas is searching for a lyrical shot to close his new book of photographs, as counterpoint to the squalor of the 'real life' represented on
the other pages. Out hunting for some bric-a-brac to decorate his
studio, he strolls across a park. The sky is cloudy, the trees disturbed,
but the scene is peaceful. Two lovers embrace in a clearing. Thomas
skips from one hiding place to another, crouching behind one tree,
then the next, taking photographs. He is intoxicated with the activity.
But the girl hears a noise and comes over to demand the film. Thomas
refuses, and returns to his studio to develop it. When he blows up the
prints, he gradually discovers that the scene he was photographing was
quite different from the idyllic tableau he thought he had seen: the
gentle rapture with which he hoped to close his brutal series of photographs, shots of the old, the poor, the desolate, the photograph that
was to be such a contrast to all this, proves to be a document revealing
murder in a London park.

This is unfolded in a thrilling sequence, to which the recent scrutiny
of photographic evidence in the Kennedy assassination lends an added
spice: in increasingly magnified blow-ups of certain prints, a body in
the grass and a gunman in the bushes emerge from the apparently in-
nocuous photographs. It is night. In a terrifying stillness, Thomas

comes to the clearing in the park. He finds the body. Returning to his studio, he discovers that all the photographs have gone. All have been taken except one, a blurred, inconclusive print which leaves him with no proof of the event at all—apart from the body. He hurries to a friend's house, and urges him to come and witness the corpse. But it is late, a party is in full swing, his friend is drunk, reluctant, and at last Thomas gives up and spends the night there, forgetting his quest. Throughout the day there have been distractions: the girl in the park trailed him to his studio and tried once again to get the film back, but settled for seduction instead; there is a painter who lives in the same studio, and his girl friend makes fruitless passes at Thomas; two aspiring cover girls sue to model clothes, and end by taking theirs off. These are insignificant dalliances, but his surrender to the party proves his undoing: he wakes late and hastens anxiously to the park, but the body has gone.

Thomas is a man who uses language mockingly, disparagingly, with the irony aimed at himself; who contradicts himself, who is content to be confusing, irritating in his words, because he knows he can tell the story of his life in pictures. He believes his photographs tell the truth. But now that the corpse has disappeared, he has no means left of telling this adventure at all. Who will believe him, without the body or the photographs? Not only his mode of expression but his mode of perception is threatened: the fallibility of his perception, made real to him when he discovered what the camera had seen and he had missed, is now endorsed by losing all the evidence of that discovery itself.

In *Deserto Rosso* Giuliana was a neurotic who demanded that her environment protect her, justify her, answer her needs; streets and houses echo her emotions. She had to learn to live with their indifference. Thomas has to learn that he is no more powerful over nature with a camera than without. The final scene is a ritual penitence: as he leaves the park, he comes upon a student rag group, all whited up as clowns. These students are glimpsed at various stages of the film, passing in the street, and we recognise them now. They are miming a game of tennis on the deserted courts. Thomas stops to watch. The ball is struck out of the court, and all the students watch its imaginary flight, in the direction, as it happens, of Thomas. When it lands, and they have mimed watching it bounce, the students gaze hopefully at Thomas. Will he mime the action of throwing it back, and let them continue their imaginary game? He does so, and the Thomas once so sure he could interpret what was real, confesses himself a doubting Thomas, a humble, ignorant Thomas. The last shot seals his loss of faith: we see him in close-up, watching the mime. And on the sound track there begins the noise of a racket striking a ball, then the return, the rally. He concedes he knows nothing: they might be playing a real game, for all he could tell. Thomas has passed, it seems, from one over-simplification to another.

Although the suspense in *Blow-Up*, admirably created but clumsily resolved, is of a murder-thriller kind unfamiliar to Antonioni fans— which is making the film a lot of friends in new quarters—the film's theme is thoroughly familiar. It is a melody already stated in the last 56 shots of *L'Eclisse*, where Antonioni's camera discovers what Thomas does in the course of *Blow-Up*—some of the unsuspected spheres of action contained in apparently familiar events. The closing sequence of *L'Eclisse* is a montage which reviews the lovers' abandoned rendez-vous, the place and objects which became the touchstones of their affair: a zebra crossing, a water-butt beside a building site, a water-sprinkler that sprays a nearby park. The climax, announced by a thunderous chord on the organ, is a close-up of the street-lamp bulb that illuminates the whole scene, in the gathering dusk.

The montage stresses two things: the indifference of the objective world whirling about the lovers' own febrile activity, and its energy, like the fan which smugly whirrs behind the exhausted, quarrelling couple in the opening scene. At the end, the zebra crossing which was the prelude to a kiss becomes a trivial stage in the routine walk home of passing businessmen; the water-spray which saw the lovers' first flirtation is casually switched off by a workman; jets pass overhead; other people watch them. The décor, the props of the love affair, prostitute themselves to other actors with less passionate designs, or continue their own activity independent of human behaviour: the twig that Vittoria dropped so poignantly (as she thought) into the water-butt to punctuate a meeting, slips into the gutter as the water flows out of a hole in the butt. The final shot, the mocking energy of electricity, indicts the dissipation of human energy, while the vitality of the objective world continues to expend its energy to scientifically assessable laws.

During the montage passers-by are scrutinised in a series of increasingly magnified close-ups. The gutter and the flowing water are treated with the same intensity. What each blow-up shows is a whole new picture: each pulsing vein in an old man's cheek is allowed autonomy by the intensification of focus; details of clinging mud and leaves form new shapes of microscopic beauty. Vittoria's response to this busy, sometimes mischievous universe is, as far as one can make out, to cope. But Thomas renounces his previous smugness for a worse smugness: the luxury of despair and renunciation of responsibility.

He believed he was wedded to reality by his camera: when he discovers that reality is unfaithful to him, that he has never possessed it completely, he renounces all conjugal rights: all reality, he meekly concedes, is appearance. Although he knows the rag students are miming their tennis match, he invents the sound of racket on ball. The way Antonioni's thesis is presented is inconsistent with both the metaphysical proposition and the physical situation. In the first place, a leap has been made between the proposition that we often settle for oversimplified explanations of an event, and the directive that all explanation is futile. Certainly, Thomas was mistaken in thinking that he had photographed a quiet afternoon; but this is not necessarily metaphysical arrogance: a telephoto lens would have solved the problem at the time, and wedded him to a more complex reality rather more satisfactorily than his nothing-is-really-real gesture at the end.

The film seems to be making the paranoiac's leap from the proposition that objective reality is largely indifferent to one's desires, which is an unobjectionable argument, to the proposition that it conspires against one. Anna's disappearance in *L'Avventura* was a mysterious one—but it permitted of certain quite specific speculations: either she drowned; or she ran away, as she had threatened to do. The absence of a conclusive solution didn't lead Sandro and Claudia to see imaginary tennis matches, or to wonder whether Anna ever existed. The same applies to *Blow-Up*. The body disappeared: well, somebody took it away. To rush to the extreme conclusion that nothing is real embraces Pirandellism, and forms a significantly different proposition to the statement that our means of observing and assessing reality are desperately limited.

If this were the gist of *Blow-Up*, there would be no need for Thomas to 'hear' the noises suggested by a student rag mime. He knows as well as we do that there is no tennis match. His camera has just unveiled to him a whole set of circumstances that his senses missed: instead of proclaiming all modes of perception invalid, which he does in the final scene, he of all people—a photographer—should not be surprised at what the camera uncovers. This is the inconsistency in the physical situation: what photographer has this kind of shock in store? As a scientist does, working in a stricter symbology than the artist, a photographer understands what a medium of communication or a mode of perception is: it is a construct, more or less fallible. And when you find it has been fallible, as Thomas does with his senses in *Blow-Up*, you do not kick the mechanism to bits and charge fuming from the laboratory. You acknowledge the error, you discover why it happened, and you set about refiring the machinery with this new information.

This is all Thomas has to do. Because he became involved in a drunken party the night before, when he reached the park the body had gone. This does not mean that the body never existed, and he can no longer trust his memory, or that the mimed tennis match is real, and he can no longer trust his senses. All it means is that he should have extracted himself from the party and pursued his objective. Thomas is blaming on the world a failure of the will. In the first place, he has mistaken an event in a public park for something other than it is; in the second place, he has allowed himself so many distractions while investigating it that the search proves fruitless. So he resigns himself to 'hearing' a mimed tennis match: it is the act of a man who avoids the truth, the act of a man who is not prepared to criticise himself.

Which brings us to why Antonioni should move from the intellectual poise of *L'Avventura* to the clumsiness of *Blow-Up,* where he has extrapolated an idea into a story without appreciating that he has changed his area of operations. And the appearance-and-reality proposition of which the film is an embodiment is not merely a tiresome cliché, but a lazy half-truth in narrative form. "All of the other films I did with my stomach, this one I did with my brain," Antonioni said recently in an interview. He used to say bad films were made with the head or the heart, good ones only with the stomach. And we are a far cry from his Chekhovian remark "I never work from an abstraction towards a story." Antonioni claims in different ways, in different interviews (and the interviews themselves are testimony to this), that he has to preserve an area of non-articulate confrontation with his work; that the pressures of film-making make a certain avoidance of analysis essential in preserving this area of spontaneity.

I dislike being asked questions about my work, he has said, because they bring me to a level of ratiocination, whereas I prefer to work on a lower level ('livello inferiore'). Naturally, in every artist the activity must relax down into the subconscious springs of inspiration once the conscious objectives have been defined; or if not the objectives, then the framework of the piece, the broad shapes. But once the area of refusal to criticise grows too large because of arrogance, or grows too intractable because of a constant threat to it, an artist is in danger of settling for the easy choice, for the contrived and the second-rate. He lets things through.

Blow-Up is unconsciously an appeal to the worst kind of intellectual sentimentality. It is a lesson in how to take the easy way out. It could become the handbook of those words-don't-ever-really-communicate and you-can't-ever-really-know-what-I'm-feeling merchants who settle for these half-truths the moment a discussion becomes demanding, in the impermeable conviction that they are bravely confronting a more challenging and subtle reality than you. They use the limitations of perception and communication as a means of avoiding responsibility, as Thomas does in *Blow-Up*. It seems that Antonioni, too, has come to regard these limitations as an excuse rather than a challenge. *Blow-Up* is not merely an intellectual wheelchair for intellectual cripples, it propagates a moral defeatism towards the challenges of living that the film's technical expertise only renders more pernicious.

The craftsmanship is indeed of a very high order. The self-conscious use of colour in *Deserto Rosso* has been left behind as an accessory of Giuliana's neuroticism and an experiment in the neurotic distortion of chromatic values. The art direction is splendid and the camerawork (Carlo Di Palma) relaxed. Antonioni's uniquely meticulous use of sound is in evidence. The rhythm of the film is rather disjointed at times, where scenes have obviously been cut very short, parts expanded, like Vanessa Redgrave's as the girl in the park, or visibly contracted, like Sarah Miles' as the painter's girl friend. The screen is dominated by David Hemmings as Thomas, and the contribution of the other actors is somewhat curtailed by their function in the story, which is to illustrate their insignificance in Thomas' life. Hemmings serves the story extremely well, playing Thomas both expressively and economically, and gaining our sympathy without blinding us to Thomas' indifference to the people around him.

The dialogue, tailored by Edward Bond from the Antonioni-Guerra screenplay, is convincing and unobtrusive; sometimes too unobtrusive —a line tending more to patois than to colloquialism, a delivery more private than intimate. The use of slang can become a restriction of expression, not a freedom; and on these occasions one suspects the director himself is more sinned against than sinning. For a film-maker working in a language other than his own, rhetoric is not the area of dramatic dialogue hardest to assess, but casual chat. In an effort not to betray unfamiliarity, underplaying is left unchecked. But these are rare lapses. Quite apart from its status as a uniquely authoritative debut in a foreign language, the film has a great deal to offer as entertainment, in the narrative, the performances, and the fluency of Antonioni's camera style.

Above all, the story is immensely exciting. Two scenes are unforgettable: the gradual discovery of the murder as the prints are blown up, and the midnight visit to the park. An Antonioni film where the plot is enthralling and the intellectual content banal will come as a shock to a lot of people, but it is deservedly bringing him a wider audience, since the handling of *Blow-Up* as a thriller alone merits it a special place in that genre.

BLOW-UP
by HUBERT MEEKER

The impression left on me by previous Antonioni films is one of eloquently composed emptiness, and a mood of sadness too diffuse to produce the sharpness of despair, in which human contact is mostly tentative and anti-climactic.

Blow-Up comes, then, with the distinct shock of departure. The bold use of color, the sharp contrasts of milieu, and the vital rhythmic shifts of cinematic pace are but the obvious surface signs of Antonioni's deeper shift of ground.

Human relationships are depicted as even more ambiguous than before, and communication more elliptical. But through these extremes, the pervasive ennui has been sharpened into divergent points of view, forming a pattern and a sense of an external, spiritual presence I don't recall feeling before.

Where selfishness was a general standard in earlier films, a refreshing pattern of giving is established in *Blow-Up*. In the opening sequence the photographer, emerging from a doss house, makes a money contribution to the boisterous rag party. In the last sequence at the tennis court, the revelers return the favor with a gift manyfold in its importance. In a sense he has earned, and must show he has earned, what they have to give. Yet the essential quality of what is bestowed on him is that it must be both earned and given.

Another important gift at the center of the film might be described as the photographer's gift to himself, except there is also an aspect of outside intervention, the operation of an external wisdom definitely beyond him at this point. It is the delivery to his studio of the propeller he had purchased at the pawn shop. It arrives in time to break up the photographer's seduction of the strange woman, a gratuitous little moment of grace protecting the innocent and delivering justice

From Film Heritage, 2 (*Spring 1967*): 7–15. *Copyright* © *1967 by* **F. A. Macklin.** *Reprinted by permission of the editor.*

unawares. (A great deal of trouble was taken with the involved and guilty Miss Redgrave to show her essential innocence in the studio surroundings, and conversely, to point up the guilt of the uninvolved and innocent Hemmings.) The propeller stops the photographer from knowing her in the cliché physical way that has become habit with him, and forces him to aim for a better understanding of her and her situation. Of course the arrival of the propeller, that fragment of the airborne, can be described as chance, but its arrival does work on them in a beneficial way, and whether one describes this chain of events as blind or omniscient, "higher" than their present consciousness or "lower," coming from the "outside" or "inside," hardly matters. The fact that a chance event can alter men's directions for the better can still be called grace, and the propeller noted as a symbol of grace.

The other gifts in the film can be described as sacrificial. The two little girls who so badly want to become models, return in the wake of Miss Redgrave's departure to find themselves suddenly needed, but in a way they didn't expect. In this chain of events as unwitting as the propeller sequence, the girls are sacrificed to Hemmings' fever, and following that debauch in the torn and crumpled purple backdrop paper, the photographer is able to return to his blow-ups with greater clarity. Where previously he thought his intervention had saved the man's life in the park, he now reads the evidence more closely and sees the shadow of murder. This is the other sacrifice. A man's life has been taken—an older man, by the way—as the culmination of some "trouble" Miss Redgrave speaks of, and in the course of events this "trouble" is passed on to a younger man whose swinging surface existence had apparently never felt the jar of such a real encounter. The "trouble" germinates in him the possibility of new life, which the film celebrates in that ritual tennis court scene. The irony, of course, is that Hemmings doesn't make the sacrifices that lead to his progress, but takes advantage of others in his quest. This doesn't seem fair, but, then, life isn't fair, and it seems part of the film's "message" that the cost of one inch of progress in a man's becoming is inordinately high, and not necessarily meted out in deserving fashion. Yet, in another sense, the cost was nothing, the sacrifices were gratuitous in that the murder and the seduction would have occurred anyway, and the photographer earns his way to the degree he is able to make something of them.

Antonioni uses some of the elements of mystery, as we find them in popular literature, to introduce Mystery, much in the same way Graham Greene has. The capsule of this technique is recorded in the artist's studio the photographer visits. Out of the profligate amount of

paint and energy the artist has expended on his canvas, it is all a waste
except for one little passage that still intrigues him, like a clue in a
mystery story as he puts it, that is worth hanging onto and makes his
life and work worth pursuing.

But it is not the mystery that captivates us in *Blow-Up*; it is its
reality, the brilliance with which Antonioni has composed fascinating
surfaces into lasting meaning. He limits himself to what is available
to the artist, what meets the eye, the intriguing and telltale surface of
life, a surface which psychologists coming out of the depths of the
unconscious are finding far more significant than they previously
thought possible. Antonioni studies what washes up to the surface of
the swinging London milieu with that combination of scientific scrutiny and a lover's sensuous care that comes naturally to the artist.
The super-authenticity of the photographer's huge warehouse studio
engulfs us in its wealth of lovely equipment and gorgeous high-fashion
colors. It also engulfs us in its make-believe free association of planes
and spaces, as illusory screens and backdrops, scenery and props, flow
into the "real" places of darkrooms and living quarters with such easy
transition.

I was absorbed in David Hemmings' work as a fashion photographer
in this make-believe lair. The first sequence in which he stalks, dominates and ravishes a lithe tigress of a model with his camera is a wonderful evocation of trade technique. That the scene is doubly enriched
with its overtones of sexuality, and on a purely animal basis, the hunt
and the kill (the hunt for the right picture?) is just as important as a
musical instrument's timbre is to the notes it plays. The overtones,
rather than detracting from the tone itself, add to its richness and
importance and accuracy. What impresses us most in this atmosphere
of sexuality is Hemmings' "cool." It is merely work and money, the
only formula he knows for achieving the "freedom" he later expresses
a desire for.

Antonioni lingers in the studio to elaborate his theme with a second
group of models, which Hemmings treats like so many animals in a
pen. We have watched him work with one model; now we watch him
with four, and Antonioni's variations provide some wonderful color-
play before Hemmings leaves his harried models in medias res to rush
off on some other tangent of his many-faceted, wheeling-dealing life,
held together by radiophone from his Rolls convertible.

There are two other important studio sequences, however. The later
one involves the two teen-age girls who have been hanging about looking for a chance to do a little modelling. At their first appearance his
approach to them is "cool"; he sees them only in professional terms
and dismisses them. But when they come back later, after Miss Red-

grave has left, it is significant that he sees them as human beings and takes them in. The action that follows is natural for him in that particular situation. He tears off their clothes, and in a wildly funny scene of childish innocence and exuberance, he ravishes them in a heap of torn purple backdrop paper. Technically it was probably the most difficult scene to photograph and put together, and the mood of innocent playfulness that comes across, in spite of our preconceptions about the deflowering of girls, is a triumph of Antonioni artistry. It is a very warm and human scene, and the mark of the photographer's "humanization" for want of a better word. But the crowning irony of the scene, and the proof that Hemmings' progress is gratuitous, is that these two debauched little girls, numb as statues, seem to harbor one disappointment: they still haven't had their pictures taken!

The pivotal studio scene concerns Hemmings' confrontation with the woman whose picture he has taken in the park embracing an older man. Although Hemmings later makes plain his interest in making pictures from life, when he discusses his book of candid photographs in the restaurant with his writer friend, his trip to the park is the one important instance of his working from life, and is sharply contrasted with his commercial studio. From the intense, op-art studio scenes with the bevy of models, Antonioni makes a careful and deliberate transition to the suburban park. The pace begins to wind down as Hemmings wheels his convertible past a long row of old buildings painted solid red, punctuated at the end by a solitary blue building, and followed by the spaciously-sited new apartment buildings in a calm tan brick. Hemmings' rummaging around in the antique shop, from which he later buys the propeller, reinforces the image of Hemmings as a man living a fragmentary existence, a collector of unusual photographic glimpses and odd isolated experiences. Isn't it significant that he never uses a movie camera, but sees life in neatly framed stills? The antique shop is also the last step in Antonioni's winding down of the pace of the film and introducing the lyrical passage in the park. The moist air glistens with pearly light, and the green of the trees and grass is exquisitely pure and fragile. Yet in contrast to the complex and sophisticated studio scenes before it, where a kind of professional security reigned, there is a subtle insecurity and sense of mounting danger in the simple purity of the park, underscored by the ominous sighing of the wind in the trees. The idyll of the strolling lovers as Hemmings stalks them also has a note of strangeness about it. We notice the woman leading the man, not to the seclusion one would suspect her to desire, but into the open light and positioning him as if according to a plan. Whatever is going on is interrupted by Hemmings' presence, and Miss Redgrave follows him back to his studio to bargain for the photos he took of her. Her plain but strong and elegant features establish her immediately as a person of more than cosmetic interest, and her anxious pacing in the studio contrasts sharply with the artificial animal movements of the model earlier on. "My private life is already in a mess," she says. "It would be a disaster if . . ." "So what!" answers Hemmings. "Nothing like a little disaster to sort things out." His flip tone of voice underscores the authenticity of her predicament by contrast. He talks about disaster while she so obviously is in its grips, and the intensity of her involvement provides the first instance in the film in which Hemmings loses his cool. His rambling conversation about the ill-defined wife who is not a wife, the children who don't exist, and their mother's easy-to-live-with qualities that make it impossible for him to live with her—all reveal that the "mess" of Hemmings' life is far different from the disaster of Miss Redgrave's. Hers comes across as something sharply defined and authentic, while his seems a vague muddle—the product of his own mindlessness. And to carefully visualize this mindlessness Antonioni purposely never sorts out the identity of the woman on the phone, or the exact role of Sarah Miles, or whether or not they are one and the same.

Nevertheless Hemmings tries to dominate Miss Redgrave by turning her into another of his models. "Not many women can stand like that," he observes. "Show me how you sit!" But she is more than a match for him. In removing her blouse and offering him sex in return for the film, she shows herself one step ahead of him and in command of the situation. But the fact that she is a real person, a vulnerable and involvable person, works against her. She suddenly finds herself involved with Hemmings, while he takes advantage of her vulnerability to give her a substitute roll of film. Only the propeller, in its timely arrival, saves her from being further seduced, and saves Hemmings from turning a real encounter into a cliché one.

The careful and exacting sequences of Hemmings developing and enlarging the pictures is exciting in its verisimilitude. I can't recall another film in which the technical aspects of a trade have been used to such powerful effect. Very little use is made of standard suspense techniques to sustain this passage. The process itself is far more interesting for the moment than the end result. Hemmings tried to make contact with Miss Redgrave by turning her into something familiar to him, another model; but now he tries to reach the truth she contains by more honest means, the only thing he really knows, the art of photography. The photographs he took in the park he keeps blowing up, larger and larger, almost "larger than life" in order to discover a clue to the mystery. At one point he sees that Miss Redgrave was setting up her friend for murder, but thinks his intrusion saved the man's life. After the intrusion of the two girls, however, he returns to the photographs, and to get even larger blow-ups takes pictures of the pictures. In this second removal from reality, the picture is so enlarged as to have lost all its quality as photography, has become a kind of coarse screen through which Hemmings sees the truth he is looking for: a ghostly image in the shrubbery pointing a gun.

Hemmings returns to the park to look for evidence of murder, and Antonioni treats his repeated climb up the long steps into the park with the feeling of a pilgrimage, the labor of a quest, his progress through the night lighted by the neon gleam of a large sign, which seems to say nothing but simply registers its presence as a true sign, a primitive emblem casting its light on this natural preserve and the vulgar cadaver it contains. The brittle skin and eyes of the corpse against the greensward that is almost black in this night scene, is terribly striking. Yet in spite of the darkness, the film preserves the essential greenness of the park, a fitting backdrop for the scene in which Hemmings has the reality of life brought home to him by the reality of death. For the swinger whose life has been one empty happening after another, at last something has happened.

From here on, images of breakdown, emptiness and death fill the screen: the shambles of Hemmings' studio as he returns to it; the soulless hysteria at the soul-rock music performance with its canned music, the breakdown of the electronic equipment, and the discarding of the broken phallus, the bridge from the ineffectual musician's guitar; and the empty bliss at the marihuana party, an urban reflection of the earlier rural scene, as it were, everyone smoking "grass" and the same perfect tranquility with the same overtones of dangerous emptiness. Even the presence of death is carried forward by the bust of that strangely incongruous 18th century gentleman, standing solid and cadaverous amid the gently floating marihuana spirits. The help Hemmings is looking for is not to be found, but apparently the consequences of his detached life are not too hard to bear. Since his friends are too far gone to help him, he takes the other alternative and joins them in their night of escapism. But in the morning the memory of the corpse must still haunt him, for he returns to confirm its presence and get some proof in the way of a photograph. By the time he arrives, however, the body is gone. The evidence for the reality he had encountered has now become invisible, spiritualized, and the only issue remaining is if Hemmings understands this and accepts it. The man who was looking for freedom through money, and had reduced others to ciphers in this formula, has now been engaged in bondage by—nothing—by an experience whose tangible counters have vanished into thin air.

Antonioni needed a very clear and unambiguous statement to close the film, and he found it in the rag party that opened the film. These gay celebrants, first seen roaring around the Economist Plaza in quick-cut contrast with the silent vagrants leaving the doss house, now come careening through the park and stop at the tennis courts to play a mimed game of tennis. Hemmings looks on with his customary detached interest, compared to the painted and absorbed faces of the students as they watch the make-believe ball batted back and forth by two of their companions. It is a fascinating sequence, so well done that we begin to believe in the invisible ball ourselves, and when one of the players hits it over the fence and gestures for Hemmings to return it, we are keenly in touch with this dilemma whose solution will bring in the last bit of evidence needed to close the film. Hemmings returns the imaginary ball, and the game goes on. His new-found faith in that invisible ground for men's sharing is reinforced by the sound track: the pock-pock of a tennis ball, like the sound of one hand clapping. The mystery is complete; not a mystery to be solved, but a mystery to be realized.

The Road to Damascus:
BLOW-UP
by JEAN CLAIR

Adapted from a short story by Julio Cortázar, *Blow-Up,* Antonioni's latest film, has excited public interest in the United States. It is not unusual to see Americans freezing in line for over an hour before getting in to the movie house. Curious also is audience-reaction according to city: if Bostonians, disconcerted and shocked, break out laughing to hide their discomfort, the more Europeanized New Yorkers, especially students and people from Greenwich Village, receive the film with welcome silence, punctuated only at the end with modest applause—a very rare reaction in France.

The reason for its success is that *Blow-Up,* which is obviously less ambitious than *Red Desert,* seems to mark the climax of a logical discourse that Antonioni has been repeating and refining since, at least, *Le Amiche.* In *Blow-Up* he reaches a point in his argument so delicate and so extreme that Antonioni seems to signify the opposite of the thesis he has been stating all along. Furthermore, he has come to a point of such vivid brightness that, like the light that St. Paul saw, the evidence in *Blow-Up* blinds us: the brightness of Antonioni's vision plunges us into total night.

In his earlier movies, studies of inertia men feel when faced with reality, one line of the movement of the film always found daylight. If, in *L'Avventura,* Sandro's and Claudia's love was incapable of resolving their personal problems, they at least remained together. And in *La Notte,* Giovanni and Lidia, knowing that their marriage would never be happy, decided not to separate. *Red Desert* ended with

From Positif, *no. 84 (May 1967): 1–6. Copyright © 1967 by Editions le Terrain Vague. English translation by Norman Silverstein. Copyright © 1970 by Norman Silverstein. Reprinted by permission of the publisher and the translator.*

Giuliana's decision not to attempt suicide any more, even though she would continue to be haunted by her neurosis. Antonioni's characters recognized facts, which Antonioni authenticated, about their lives. With *Blow-Up*, he transcends the stage of showing things as they are in order to reach the stage of ecstasy. We pass beyond the *stans* of things-as-they-are in favor of *ecstasis*, the soul's going out from the body—the stage of the deprivation of the real. Until *Blow-Up*, his characters *knew* and accepted the knowledge that they knew. They knew and accepted that their Pauline adventures across a desert ended in night. This knowledge was like the promise of salvation. But when, as in *Blow-Up*, there is no longer any evidence to be derived from fact, which at least has an immediacy—fact which because of its abrupt violence you can no longer grasp—of what use is it to search, to speak, and to know?

Indeterminancy reigns. In *Blow-Up*, the most naked reality has a hidden side that makes us slip into the domain of the ambiguous and the obscure, without our retaining anything at all of reality itself. In still-life paintings, as in Dutch interiors, painters express through an absolute simplicity of persons and objects another, more fundamental reality. So in this transparent, crystal-clear, almost linear film, Antonioni answers for us the essential question of our presence in the world and its meaning. In earlier films the question concerned the phenomenology of existence; in *Blow-Up*, the question is at the root-level of an ontological quest. Antonioni has never before ventured so far into allegory or toward the expression of the inexpressible. For this reason, many American critics have judged with severity Antonioni's abuse, as they see it, of both symbolism and sophistication.

Brilliantly acted by David Hemmings, the hero is a London fashion photographer—perfect example of that new Carnaby Street generation called "pop," "mod," "turned on," or "hip." He seems to be the curious result of cross-breeding the American beat generation and the Edwardian dandy. Aged 26 or 27, he owns all that one can desire. He drives a Rolls. He has the option to abuse sex and marijuana. He can seduce the most beautiful London models. Yet he always retains a sort of intermittent detachment proper to him and his kind. As the *Time* critic put it, he is the sort of "fungus that can grow freely in a rotting society."

The earlier scenes show several examples of social rot, reminding the moviegoer of Fellini's sense of the grotesque. On the one hand, a group of beaux-arts students in costumes, their faces covered with white powder, descend, screaming and laughing, on London streets as deserted as Eliot's *Waste Land*. Meanwhile, a group of silent unemployed leaves a night shelter for a hiring office. These short scenes, in parallel editing, suffice to define social reality in contemporary England—for the young, what they will soon be calling their Flaming Youth; for adults, a reality of social crisis and unemployment. From the group of bums the face of the photographer detaches itself [Plate I]. He has spent the night with them to take pictures of these wrecks—remarkable and cruel photos we shall see later on. He knows his job. He keeps "cool." In the thirties, to be a photographer meant Stieglitz, Steichen, or Dorothea Lange—to be witness of a certain reality, to share it, at least to believe in it. Today, to be a photographer is rather to stand before that same reality, which has become foreign, even exotic, and to assume the role of frozen indifference in order to draw from it that perfect objectivity which, paradoxically, yields a surplus of realism even when that reality is being denied. So, with the masquers and the unemployed as a sort of emblem, Antonioni establishes, as if it were a game, the problem of art and life, of illusion and reality.

Nevertheless, like earlier Antonioni heroes, the young photographer will also find himself on the Road to Damascus. Wandering about, he enters a London park. Ignoring a strange fat woman in uniform who is busily scavenging, a shot nine out of ten photographers without thinking twice would have taken, he photographs first some pigeons, then a pair of lovers. The girl, Vanessa Redgrave, notices him and begs him to give her the roll of film. Following him to his studio, she offers to make love to him if he agrees to give her the negatives. At first he refuses. Then he tricks her by giving her unused film. Later, when he develops the photographs, he is struck by her shocked look on one of them. He blows up a detail and proves that, unknown to himself, he has been witness to a murder. Her partner in lovemaking has been killed by the girl's true lover, who was hidden in the bushes. A trap is beginning to close around the photographer. His camera, which enabled him to avoid reality, has returned him to it in a most brutal manner.

And what is reality? It is the grainy jumble of black and white dots on sensitive paper, which, when blown up, yields an abstract diagram. The dots of this part stand for the hidden killer and of that part for the stretched-out corpse. Among the photographer's friends is a painter who began his career with representative painting but turned to the "dripping" technique. Standing before a "dripping" canvas, he has told the photographer, "It's like a detective story. I'm looking for the key to the mystery without finding it." Later, when the painter's girl friend is standing in front of the photographer's blow-ups, she has almost the same reaction. "It's like his painting," she says. "You can't recognize anything."

Such is the ambiguity of art: to fix upon and to blow-up a piece of reality which, howsoever steadied, escapes us at the very moment we are participating in it. (Antonioni's greatest skill in the film lies in his making the moviegoer share the very first view of the crime and to be no more aware of it than is the hero.) A work of art eludes us by its becoming an abstraction. Therefore, by converting reality into abstraction, art *betrays* reality in the double sense that we can use the word *betray:* it "betrays" somethingof reality, *i.e.,* it represents, if only in outlines, something real; it also falsifies life. Contemporary science has also known this kind of impasse. And who has not had the impression of trickery that is almost unbearable before one of Seurat's bathers? The bather's body, so real from a certain distance, her flesh so handsomely and permanently rendered, becomes, as soon as you move nearer to the canvas to grasp her better. . . . She dissolves, she scatters into the dust of colored spots, *taches* suddenly deprived of any meaning.

That evening the photographer returns to the park to *verify* the murder. For the first time, with his naked eye and for no more than an instant—he feels the compulsive impact of a reality: the corpse, already stiff, its eyes open, is really there. Ill at ease, the photographer returns home where he finds his girl friend stretched out like some famous painting, like the body on the grass in the blow-up, suffocating and groaning under the painter's sexual thrusts. This vision of love is as dizzying and as unbearable, perhaps as unreal to our conception, as the vision of death.[1]

Early the next morning, without having dared to alert the police or even to get advice from his friends who, during a party have been comforting themselves with alcohol and drugs, the photographer returns to the park for the third and last time. He hopes to take a photograph that will establish the reality of the murder. Instead of the corpse, he finds nothing but a plot of grass looking as if nothing has lain on it.

The band of white-powdered students takes over a nearby tennis court and with imaginary tennis balls and imaginary rackets begin to mime a tennis match. Interested in spite of himself and recovering his professional habit of being a voyeur, the photographer approaches them. When the "ball" is hit over the fence and stops at his feet, he hesitates a moment. Then, while the players are looking at him and waiting, he makes believe he is picking up the "ball" and returning it. We hear the ball bounce back. Given an absolute indeterminacy of what is real, the only possible way to act is to multiply illusion by

[1] To my knowledge, *Blow-Up* is the first commercial film to show even for a brief instant the completely naked body of a woman, her sex slightly exposed.

illusion and willingly to accept appearance as reality. The work of art is both the tree that hides the forest of reality from us and the screen that shelters us from the void of reality.

Filmgoers may find the allegory either much too complicated or exaggeratedly simple. Antonioni's genius rests on the fact that he has presented a very abstract subject with such concrete and sensitive images as he has prepared us to expect from him. Chief among these images is the physical reality of the park, conveyed to us by the noise of wind among the leaves. When the film is released in Paris, there will be critics who will notice the thematic use of the color violet, the color of the Passion, from the mauve turban of a Hindu on a London street to a garnet-red dawn over the Thames, as beautiful as a Bonnard painting, along with the purple screens that serve the photographer in his studio.

Reasons enough to suppose and to hope that *Blow-Up* will receive one of the grand prizes at the next Cannes Festival.

THE BLOW-UP
by MAX KOZLOFF

The Blow-Up is not only a film which deals mysteriously with photographic enlargements; it also emerges as a magnification of Antonioni's whole repertoire of themes, now incised with a feverishness that borders on hallucination. Without doubt, most of his earlier perceptions are present: of the insufficiency and transience of human affection, of chilled eroticism, of the muteness of objects, of intermittent hysteria, and a sundered social fabric. Into this always pessimistic but understated matrix of themes, he introduces such sharp awareness of the nominally bright-eyed mod London locale, that its various strata burst more freshly into recognition than in many a film by a native director.

But none of this is as central to the work as its concern for blending degrees of anxious dream into an almost documentary reality. The fact that the protagonist here, an artist figure like such earlier Antonioni "heroes" as the architect and the writer, is a photographer, involved with a stylish *recording* of his own scene, only heightens Antonioni's enigma. This photographer has a devilish flair for capturing the decorative hanky-panky, the high or mean extravagance of gleaming English camp—he is, after all, one of its creatures. But when it comes to catching real life on the wing—and as he (and we) suspect, a particularly dire instance of it—his lens unaccountably fails. More than this, there is an equation made between the hectic gropings of the photographer in his search after truth, and the equivocations of the movie camera itself. So that, in a whirl of subliminal hints and peripheral vignettes (never in themselves parenthetical: the camera may skip ahead, but never jumps to the side of the action), one is made to doubt whether certain events occur in the character's imagination

From Film Quarterly, *Vol. 20, no. 3, pp. 28–31. Copyright © 1967 by the Regents of the University of California. Reprinted by permission of The Regents and the author.*

or one's own. Not only does a paucity of narrative evidence contrast with a richness of behavioral provocation, but cinematic means oscillate subtly in their truth values. *Blow-Up,* in the end, is a psyche-out.

That Antonioni has always been more interested in probing the psychological tropisms of people than explaining their actual situations or narrating the events which make up their lives, is evident from all his earlier work. Here he seems to be telling us, not only that the "events"—fragments of social or sexual interchanges—are all that we can know about human psychology, but that they themselves are subject to canceling interpretations. Yet the disbelief which they incite is as hesitant as his whole view of human impingements is tentative. There would be, perhaps, nothing new in this Pirandellesque situation, were it not for Antonioni's emphatic reliance on the visual. What is being said, what is being exchanged, between characters, is less revealing than is how they might be *observed.* The famous "inability to communicate" which has supposedly marked his personages, far from being an indigenous trait, is nothing more than a reflex of Antonioni's skepticism about narrative as a cinematic vehicle of expression. Hence, the real tension that symptomizes this, as well as his preceding films, is the abortiveness of an obsession with states of mind that can be materialized only through a revelation of surfaces and silences. There is a built-in acknowledgement of the inadequacy of photography to trap these states; but for that very reason, a correspondingly more studied amplification of the formal means to surmount that inadequacy. In the largest sense, then, Antonioni is a director of yearning.

Doubtless, *Blow-Up* is his most personal film to date because it mirrors, or better, almost allegorizes, his own desire and predicament as an artist. It would have been hard to foresee his path after *Red Desert,* which was the most excruciating rendering of his spiritual disorientation—and of a certain languid mannerism—that he has yet given us. Now, in retrospect, a hint can be seen in his development of color. *Red Desert* had a sulky cosmetic quality: chocolates and cinnamon greys, relieved by peaches, bleached blues, and blondes. All this was redolent of the chronic disturbance that the director perceived in his special vision of the female world. More than that, when it did not recall Pontormo or Rosso, it registered an affinity with the muted tones of *Pittura Metafisica,* not di Chirico so much (except, of course, in his spatial sensitivity) but Carrà and Morandi. (That Antonioni was born five years earlier, but at the same place, Ferrara, as *Pittura Metafisica,* is perhaps more than a coincidence. Of these painters, the art historian Werner Haftmann says that their "resurgent sense of their *italianità* conjured up the ghosts of Giotto, Masaccio,

Uccello, and their archaic idea of the solidity of things. With their universality, the works of these masters seemed to embody the *principio italiano,* its serene magic forms, its vision of a sublime 'second reality.' " *Blow-Up* too, is in color, but its palette, with significant exceptions, is in black and white.

Not for one minute would this have been anticipated as a chromatic response to London. And it has in common with *Red Desert* only its sense of a retreat from full-blown or heavily saturated coloration—with the difference that one now views sensuality in a modal rather than a minor key. Practically at the opening, we see Negro nuns dressed in white, one of the first of many reversals of expected hue. The thematic crucible of the film, the photographer's studio, a marvelous, split-level, rambling warren of catwalks, settings, and darkrooms, reaches the apogee of colorlessness in its white phones, statues, chairs, and paintings (of which, one, a luminous globe on a dark ground, is reminiscent of the end of *Eclipse*). The streets of the city, too, tinted by silvery half light, seem more than usually bled of intermediate varieties of color, which makes the few reds that punctuate the differing sequences, and, of course, the green park, exceptionally vivid. All this is delivered in a quite fine-grained, almost velvety surface that accentuates contrasts as crisp as those in *Red Desert* were chalky. Expectedly, then, the color symbolism of the two films is radically opposed.

Where such an element as the painted white vegetables in the Ravenna street symptomized a kind of social desiccation, the whites in *Blow-Up,* together with their black opposites, are like alter egos, or possibly "negatives," of reality. Nowhere is this more evident than in the critical episode in which the photographer (David Hemmings), piqued by his unwitting subject, the girl who has pursued him from the park (Vanessa Redgrave), sets about developing and magnifying the voyeuristic shots that he has kept for himself. Born in the strange gorgeousness of the darkroom glow, these blow-ups, still glistening with their reifying chemicals, are pinned up and scrutinized. Each time Hemmings increases the scale of enlargement, he gains dimension but loses definition. It is a panic search for something hidden—a face, a gun barrel, a body—which the increasingly coarsened, black-and-white microstructure is *forced* to yield. A neighbor to whom he shows his results sees in them only a resemblance to her lover's spatter paintings. Earlier, this very painter had complained that he could not "hold on" to his images, and that one form that did emerge was "like a clue in a detective story." Antonioni, we know, had painted foliage, and God knows what else, in *Blow-Up*—surreptitious enactment of the mutability of art and nature. But more than that, it is a camouflage of realities which are less accessible than the vicarious. The true anxiety—and fascination—for the viewer is to recall, in time, a park tableau that exists for him only in fragmented, color-drained, stilled form, impossible to piece together. For an age haunted by the pink and black blurs in the Zapruder film, this quest is not without a certain horror. When the scene in Antonioni's movie again mutely appears, this time viewed close up, the secret it may have contained is irretrievably lost, but the natural *presence* is, by contrast, so overwhelming and uncanny that it is impossible to speak of mere sensory confirmation. In a sense, it had become more "real" for us in its earlier shadowy form; now, it is simply more tangible. The one comparably radiant inset in *Red Desert* was that of a girl swimming in the bluest of Mediterraneans, a fantasy more corporeal than any of the earthly doings of the action proper. With inspired perversity, Antonioni shows that, either broken down or "complete," in black and white or color, perception homes in the substratum of photography, which is never so mechanistic as to assure one of what one is seeing. Or better, how one is to interpret it.

This optional kind of visibility dominates *Blow-Up* so much (without the director claiming to be responsible for it, however) that the condition of the social encounters it reveals is altogether colored by it. These encounters fall roughly under three categories: frustration, duplicity, and indifference. The camera as an instrument for making an almost obscene kind of love, at once exhibitionistic and thwarted, is witnessed in Hemmings' photo seduction of a model. Photography as a means of picturing a lyrical tryst turns out to be an eavesdropping on a possible murder. The studio, normally an environment of glossy style and high fashion, emerges as a setting for abortive, teasing sex, and nymphet hysteria. Significantly, none of these actions is *shown* as completable, or in its entirety.

As for duplicity, the young photographer himself is a paragon of it. For example, he is first seen acting as a bum in an institution for derelicts(!). In rapid succession, he becomes a voyeur (which is his, and for the time being, our métier, too), pretends (?) that he has a wife, and cheats Redgrave out of the film she had come for. Less consciously, he may be a creature of uncertain sexuality: stifled by beautiful women, and passive or evasive when they offer themselves to him. As played remarkably by Hemmings, he is febrile, autocratic, capricious, and, outside the illusory professional world of which he is a master, completely at a loss. The largest equivocation, though, may be Antonioni's, who conceives his own stand-in to be simultaneously aggressive and timid, faltering toward a morality for which his job does not equip him. More purposefully attuned to his work than Antonioni's earlier male characters, the photographer is also more lost, more abandoned. Not only is he just as incapable of giving, as he is of inspiring love, but he is a victim imprisoned within the glass walls of his strategies of deceit. How illustrative of the man's pathos is Tom Rakewell's lament from Auden and Kallman's libretto to Stravinsky's "The Rake's Progress":

> Always the quarry that I stalk
> Fades or evades me, and I walk
> An endless hall of chandeliers
> In light that blinds, in light that sears,
> Reflected from a million smiles
> All empty as the country miles
> Of silly wood and senseless park;
> And only in my heart—the dark.[1] [Plate VI.]

It is necessary to say that indifference is also a curious leitmotif within *Blow-Up,* and one of its most pungent social comments, as well. Among the crisscrossing overlooks into the London milieu—peace marches, dope parties, and discotheques—energy itself seems drugged into cyclical and meaningless repetition. It is as if Dante had been hanging around the world of rock and roll, and found it to have been damned by the emptiness of its enthusiasm, and its pointless extravagance: surrogates rather than sources of feeling. As a result, this is a world that cannot negotiate or sustain social interaction, and a scene whose members cannot help themselves. Above all, in this ambiance of deteriorated affect, no one possesses enough credibility to generate concern over the possible loss of a fellow human being. Unable to convince any friend that there had been a murder, the photographer comes to doubt his own perceptions, and begins to lose touch in the envelope mime which ends the film. Yet it is only his nostalgia for freedom, or rather, impulse towards the authentic, and Redgrave's desperation, which fleetingly break the general ennui. As for the latter, Moravia has described it quite well: "We spend most of our lives pulling bits of plaster off walls—in other words, contemplating reality without either entering into or understanding it. This is a perfectly normal condition, which leads many people to passivity, to resignation, to something like complacent hedonism. But sometimes, as with Antonioni's characters, the refusal to accept this condition, with its absence of communication and its automatism, leads to anguish." (1961) In its pithy glimpses of

[1] From *The Rake's Progress* by Igor Stravinsky. Copyright © 1949, 1950, 1951 by Boosey and Hawkes Inc. Reprinted by permission.

this anguish, *Blow-Up* certainly achieves *dramatic* tension; but this tension, now leaving the earlier work behind, transcends the rather familiar ideas above, through its *cinematic* formulation of enigma.

Some last words about the formal construction, the working out of the enigma. As leisurely (though many-incidented) in its approach to climax as, say, Hitchcock's *Rear Window* (whose story it resembles), *Blow-Up*'s central event submerges mysteriously within a welter of unforeseen "data," and larger themes. Uniformly brisk throughout, the film is punctuated by repetitions, or rather, analogies. The whole piece is a network of proposals of action and dissipations of "evidence." For every addition, there is a cancellation, in almost a noncumulative, entropic format. Moreover, the focus is on, not so much what will, but what *has* happened—so that the progression of episodes is always being dragged back towards unnoticed clues—and an eventual stillpoint. If this is the greatest "reversal" of the work, its conflict of action and re-call, initiating differing time senses, it nevertheless presents itself as one homogeneous weave of consciousness, in which observation is always of something nominally "out there." On a particular level, examples of "reversal" are the presence of the blow-ups, and their theft (?), the sight of the body and its later absence, the attraction of the artist's mistress to the photographer and her subsequent turning away from him, and the fight for the broken guitar followed by its abandonment on the street. And all these divergent happenings are integrated or spread, some near, some further from each other, with such intelligence that while they stop us to beg questions, they do not halt the flow of general inquiry or draw inordinate attention to themselves. Even sound, always exquisitely articulated, possesses the same rhyme, as when one notices the similarity between the breathing of lovers in inter-course, and the hissing of wind in the trees. Few can vie with Antonioni in his epigrammatic isolation of "throwaway" detail, which nevertheless lingers in the memory. But the most startling coup along these lines is the overture and finale of *Blow-Up,* both dominated by the presence of some rather un-English mimes (whose make-up is reminiscent of that of the fashion mannikins). That they play imaginary tennis at the end has already been prepared for us by the sight of a real tennis match earlier in the film. But when Hemmings enters their game by return-ing their illusory ball, he hears (who knows what he sees?) its distant thuds on rackets. The last shot, the longest in the entire picture, shows him wandering far beneath the camera's gaze, pitiably reduced in such a way as to suggest that just possibly the whole film up to then had been a species of blow-up. It is a terrifying implication. But no question can be more pertinent than to decide whether it is a liberating one.

ESSAYS

Three Encounters with
BLOW-UP
by ARTHUR KNIGHT

To date I have had three exposures to Michelangelo Antonioni's *Blow-Up*, each under drastically different circumstances and with drastically different audiences. The first was at a special preview offered by Metro-Goldwyn-Mayer at the Directors Guild Theatre in Hollywood, intended primarily for industry people. They hated it. It was almost as if Antonioni had insulted them personally by making a picture that departed so radically from conventional story patterns and techniques. Famous directors, writers and producers buzzed from group to group, drink in hand, asking each other what the picture was all about, and shrugging humorously when an immediate answer was not forthcoming. Obviously, the feeling was that both they and Metro had been had by an Italian upstart who had made his film deliberately obscure as a kind of spiteful, anti-Hollywood joke. Some admitted that the script's central situation—the sudden discovery of an unsuspected corpse in a photographic enlargement—was quite ingenious; but then, they added, think what Hitchcock might have done with such an idea!

For my second viewing, Metro was kind enough to let me borrow the film to show to a graduate class in film criticism that I conduct at U.S.C. When the lights came on, the ensuing animated discussion lasted almost two hours—and could have gone longer except that it was getting on toward midnight. This group, most of them in their twenties, far from asking what it all meant, began at once to dig into Antonioni's imagery to find meanings of their own. The symbol of the camera fascinated them as the perfect device to suggest the alienation of *Blow-Up*'s youthful protagonist; his only contact with reality is through his view-

From Film Heritage, *2 (Spring 1967): 3–6. Copyright © 1967 by F. A. Macklin. Reprinted by permission of the editor and the author.*

finder—and then only in blacks and whites. (To emphasize this, one student acutely observed, Antonioni drastically altered his palette from the greyed pastels of *Red Desert* to the vivid, heightened colorations of *Blow-Up*'s park foliage and the studio interiors.) Through this bright world the photographer walks like a zombie, blind unless a camera is strapped about his neck. The one time that he appears without it is when he revisits the clearing at night and discovers there the corpse. His immediate reaction is to run home for his camera. Only in a photograph does reality become meaningful for him.

Naturally, the film's equivocal ending came in for considerable discussion. Like the photographic blow-ups that transform an idyll in a park into a scene of dread and horror [Plate XI], the clown-like characters with their ball-less tennis match intriguingly pose Antonioni's central question: What is reality? What is truth? What is illusion? Some found the final scene, in which the photographer scoops up the imaginary ball and tosses it back over a fence to the players, a further evidence of the young man's fundamental inability to differentiate between illusion and reality—and hence, by extension, the metaphoric representation of a problem of our time. Others pointed to the fact that, once he has thrown the ball to the players, for the first time he (and we) *hear* the twang of the rackets and its soft thud on the clay court. Curiously, by this time the raggle-taggle clowns, first glimpsed racketing through the streets of London in an over-crowded jeep, have acquired a new significance. Whereas earlier they had seemed to be outsiders, grotesques who pursue their own pleasures without thought or care for the life of London's ordinary citizens, in a later appearance they are seen mingling in the march of some anti-war demonstrators; and by the end of the film, so drear and drab and degenerate are the people who surround the young photographer (who moves through much of the film almost as an automaton, dead behind the eyes), that the clowns seem to represent life itself. In this sense, when the hero joins their game, one has the feeling of a final affirmation, that he is aligning himself with people who are joyfully alive and not part of his shadowy black-and-white world of photographs.

The significance of this discussion, for me, lay less in the students' ultimate interpretation of the film (or better, *interpretations,* for there were probably as many viewpoints expressed as there were students in the class), than in the fact that all of them were trying to arrive at Antonioni's meaning through a close scrutiny of Antonioni's techniques. They were intrigued first on the visual level, and sought to adduce his intent in terms of what they *saw*. They were working directly with the images, not with the abstractions of a literary theme—which may have been why it was often so difficult for them to put into words their precise reactions to the film, but is also a fair measure of *Blow-Up*'s stature as an authentic cinematic experience.

My third encounter with the film came during the Broadcasting and Film Commission of the National Council of Churches' annual award deliberations just a few days after our classroom discussion. Each year the National Council presents a prize to pictures that "portray with honesty and compassion the human situation, in which man is caught in tension between his attempts to realize the full potential of his humanity." In other, less churchly circles this would probably be termed the "mature" category. As the only layman on the nominations panel, I was not only delighted but amazed when *Blow-Up* came under lengthy and serious consideration. "The most moral film I have seen in years," several of the Reverends contended. Others were willing to agree to the film's fundamental morality, but were nevertheless disturbed by its frequent nudity and explicit sexual activity. They observed that it was perhaps the most cheerless sex that the screen has ever presented (a point that Antonioni obviously had very much in mind as indicative of the inner deadness of his hero), but they felt that in the deliberate obscurantism of the film, this point might be lost to wider audiences. Their first responsibility, they emphasized, was to their congregations, not to the film medium. I trust I am betraying no confidence when I report that, following a prolonged discussion over *Blow-Up*, *Who's Afraid of Virginia Woolf?* was given the National Council's award with almost no opposition. *Virginia Woolf* might well have sparked a lively controversy had it been alone and out front; but in the shadow of Antonioni's film, it seemed almost conventional, almost safe.

And here is perhaps the real significance of *Blow-Up*. I suspect that future historians will recognize it as important and germinal a film as *Citizen Kane, Open City* and *Hiroshima, Mon Amour*—perhaps even more so. For in a curious, complex way, Antonioni is getting back to first principles. Like Griffith, he wants to make you *see,* to absorb quickly, intuitively, the visual symbols that are semaphored from the screen. For an increasingly eye-minded generation, it is an ideal approach. The very ambiguity of his imagery in *Blow-Up* the young people find stimulating, provocative, exciting. Small wonder that Hollywood's film makers, still wedded to the written script derived from a literary source, find *Blow-Up* so difficult to accept. It opens vistas for a kind of cinema that they can neither understand nor hope to emulate. But by being so far out in front, it provides the umbrella under which undoubtedly more such films can and will be made—and is, therefore, not merely a challenge but a threat to much of what exists today.

A Year with BLOW-UP:
Some Notes
by STANLEY KAUFFMANN

I first saw *Blow-up* in early December 1966, and in the months since, I have broadcast, written, and lectured considerably about it. Here are some notes on the experience.

Quite apart from its intrinsic qualities, *Blow-up* is an extraordinary social phenomenon. It is the first film from abroad by a major foreign director to have immediate national distribution. It was seen here more widely and more quickly than, for instance, *La Dolce Vita* for at least two reasons: it was made in English and it was distributed by a major American company. There are other reasons, less provable but probably equally pertinent: its mod atmosphere, its aura of sexuality, and, most important, its perfect timing. The end of a decade that had seen the rise of a film generation around the country was capped with a work by a recognized master that was available around the country.

So this was the first time in my experience that a new film had been seen by virtually everyone wherever I talked about it. Usually the complaint had been (by letter) after a published or broadcast review, "Yes, but where can we see the picture?" Or, after a talk at some college not near New York, "But it will take years to get here, if ever," or "We'll have to wait until we can rent a 16-millimeter print." With *Blow-up,* people in Michigan and South Carolina and Vermont knew —within weeks of the New York premiere—the film that was being discussed. This exception to the usual slow-leak distribution of foreign films had some interesting results.

A happy result was that people had seen this picture at the local Bijou. Before many of them had seen (say) Antonioni only in film courses and in film clubs. This one they had seen between runs of *How to Steal a Million* and *Hombre*. To those in big cities this may seem commonplace, but in smaller communities it was a rare event and had some good effects. To some degree it alleviated culture-vulturism and snobbism; *everyone* in Zilchville had seen *Blow-up*, not just the elite; so happily, there was no cachet simply in having seen it. Further, the fact of seeing it at the Bijou underscored those elements in the film medium of popular mythos that are valuable and valid—all those undefined and undefinable powers of warm communal embrace in the dark.

But there were some less happy results of the phenomenon. There was a good deal of back-formation value judgment. Because *Blow-up* was a financial success, it could not really be good, I heard, or at least it proved that Antonioni has sold out. We heard the same thing about Bellow and *Herzog* when that book became a best-seller. The parallel holds further in that *Blow-up* and *Herzog* seem to me flawed but utterly uncompromised works by fine artists. I confess I got a bit weary of pointing out that to condemn a work because it is popular is exactly as discriminating as praising it because it is a hit.

Another discouraging consequence. Much of the discussion reflected modes of thought inculcated by the American academic mind, particularly in English departments. Almost everywhere there were people who wanted to discuss at length whether the murder in *Blow-up* really happened or was an illusion. Now Antonioni, here as before, was interested in ambiguities; but ambiguities in art, like those in life, arise only from unambiguous facts—which is what makes them interesting. Anna in *L'Avventura* really disappeared; the ambiguities in morality arise from that fact. The lover in *Blow-up* was really killed; the ambiguities in the hero's view of experience would not arise without that fact. (A quick "proof" that the murder was real: If it were not, why would the girl have wanted the pictures back? Why would the photographer's studio have been rifled? Why would we have been shown the pistol in the bushes? Some have even suggested that the corpse we see is a dummy, or a live man pretending. But Hemmings touches it.) This insistence on anteater nosings in the film seemed much less a reflection on *Blow-up* than on an educational system—a system that mistakes factitious chatter for analysis.

On the other hand, an art teacher in a Nashville college told me, while driving me to the airport, that *Blow-up* had given him a fulcrum with which to jimmy his previously apathetic students into *seeing*:

seeing how the world is composed, how it is taken apart and re-composed by artists. In his excitement he almost drove off the road twice.

The script is by Antonioni and his long-time collaborator Tonino Guerra, rendered in English by the young British playwright Edward Bond. It was suggested by a short story of the same name by the Argen-tinian author, resident in France, Julio Cortázar. Comparison of the script and story is illuminating.

In the story the hero is an Argentine translator living in Paris—only an amateur photographer. One day while out walking, he photographs what he thinks is a pick-up—of a youth by an older woman. There is an older man sitting in a parked car nearby. After the picture is taken, the youth flees, the woman protests, and the man in the car gets out and protests, too. Later, studying the picture, the hero sees (or imagines he sees) that the woman was really procuring the youth for the man in the car and that the fuss over the photograph gave the youth a chance to escape. It is a story of the discovery of, in Cortázar's view, latent horror, the invisible immanence of evil. (It is incidentally amus-ing that the photographer has no such horror when he thinks that the woman is seducing the boy for herself.)

Antonioni retains little other than the device of subsequently dis-covering in a photograph what was really happening at that moment. He makes the hero a professional photographer, thus greatly intensify-ing the meaning of the camera in his life. By changing from the pre-sumption of homosexuality to the fact of murder, Antonioni not only makes the discovered event more viable dramatically, he shifts it mor-ally from the questionable to the unquestionable. At any time in history homosexuality has varied, depending on geography, in shades of good and evil. Murder, though more blinkable at some times and in some places than others, will be an evil fact so long as life has value.

Most important, Antonioni shifts the moral action from *fait accompli* to the present. His hero does not discover that he has been an agent of good, in a finished action. His dilemma is now.

With his recent films Antonioni has suffered, I think, from two pro-fessional failings of critics. The first has been well described in a pene-trating review of *Blow-up*, by Robert Garis (*Commentary*, April 1967). Garis notes that Henry James's public grew tired of him while he was inconsiderate enough to be working out his career and sticking to his guns; that Beckett, after the establishment of *Waiting for Godot* as a masterpiece, has been writing other beautiful and authentic plays quite similar to *Godot,* innocently unaware of that urgent necessity to move on, to find new themes and styles, that is so obvious to some of his critics . . . If it is regrettable to see the public wearing out new fashions in art as fast as automobiles, it is detestable to see criticism going along with this, if not actually leading the charge. The Antonioni case is like Beckett's but intensified. There has been the same puzzled annoyance with an artist who keeps on thinking and feeling about themes that everyone can see are worn out—themes like "lack of communication" or "commitment." There has been the same eagerness to master a difficult style and then the same relapse into boredom when that style turns out to be something the artist really takes seriously because that's the way he really sees things.

Another point grows out of this. This impatience with artists who are less interested in novelty than in deeper exploration leads to critical blindness about subtle graduations *within* an artist's "territory." We saw a gross example of this blindness last year in the theater when Harold Pinter's *The Homecoming* was shoved into the "formless-fear" bag along with his earlier plays. The fact that Pinter had shifted focus, that he was now using his minute, vernacular, almost-Chinese ritualism to scratch the human cortex for comic purposes, not for *frisson,* this was lost on most reviewers who were just feeling comfy at finally having "placed" Pinter.

So with Antonioni. He's the one who deals with alienation and despair, isn't he? So the glib or the prejudiced have the pigeon-hole all ready. Obviously the temper of Antonioni, like that of any genuine artist, is bound to mark all his work; but even in his last film *Red Desert,* as it seemed to me, he had pushed into new areas of his "territory," was investigating the viability of hope, and had—without question—altered the rhythms of his editing to underscore a change of inquiry (not of belief). The editing is altered even further in *Blow-up.* For instance, the justly celebrated sequence in which the hero suspects and then finds the murder in the photograph is quite unlike anything Antonioni has done before, in its accelerations and retards within a cumulative pattern. And the theme, too, seems to me an extension, a fresh inquiry, within Antonioni's field of interest. Here his basic interest seems to be in the swamping of consciousness by the conduits of technology [Plate IX]. The hero takes some photographs of lovers, and thinks he has recorded a certain experience of which he is conscious; but, as he learns subsequently, his technology has borne in on him an experience of which he was not immediately aware, which he cannot understand or handle. He is permanently connected with a finished yet permanently unfinished experience. It seems to me a good epitome of same-size man *vis-a-vis* the expanding universe.

There are concomitant themes. One of them is success—but success *today,* which is available to youth as it has never been. The hero has money, and the balls that money provides in a money-society, about twenty years earlier than would have been the general case twenty years ago; and he is no rare exception. Yet his troubles in this film do not arise from his money work but out of his "own" work, the serious work he does presumably out of the stings of conscience. (What else would drive a fashion-world hero to spend the night in a flophouse?) He can handle the cash cosmos; it is when he ventures into himself, leaves commissioned work and does something of his own, that he gets into trouble.

Along with this grows the theme of youth itself. This world is not only filled with but dominated by youth, in tastes and tone. (There are only two non-youths of prominence in the film. One, a nasty old clerk in an antique shop, resents the youth of the hero on sight. The other, a middle-aged lover, gets murdered.) The solidarity of youth is demonstrated in the hero's compunction to "prove" his strange experience to *his friends.* When one of his friends, the artist's wife, suggests that he notify the police of the murder (and her suggestion is in itself rather diffident), he simply doesn't answer to the point, as if law and criminality were outside the matter to him. Ex-soldiers say they can talk about combat only with other ex-soldiers. The communion of generations is somewhat the same. The hero doesn't want Their police; he wants certification by his friends.

Color is exquisite in Antonioni's films, and it is more than decor or even commentary; it is often chemically involved in the scene. In the shack in *Red Desert,* the walls of the bunk in which the picnickers lounge are bright red and give a highly erotic pulse to a scene in which sex is only talked about. In *Blow-up* the hero and two teen-age girls have a romp on a large sheet of pale purple-lavender paper that cools a steamy little orgy into a kind of idyll.

This is the first feature that Antonioni has made outside Italy, and it shows a remarkable ability to cast acutely in a country where he does not know the corps of working actors intimately. (He discovered David Hemmings in the Hampstead Theatre Club "off-Broadway.") It also shows a remarkable ability to absorb and redeploy the essences of a foreign city without getting either prettily or grimly picturesque. But there are three elements in this film that betray some unease—an unease attributable perhaps to the fact that he was "translating" as he went, not only in language but also in experience.

The first is the plot-strand of the neighboring artist and his wife. (Several people asked during the year, why I call her his wife and not his girl friend. Answer: She wears a wedding ring. If it is unduly naive to assume from this that the artist is her husband, it seems unduly sophisticated to assume that he is not.) This element has the effect of patchwork, as if it had not been used quite as intended or as if it were unfulfilled in its intent. The relationship between them and the hero is simply not grasped. The poorest scene in the entire film is the one in which the wife (Sarah Miles) visits the hero's studio after he has seen her making love with her husband. It is wispy and scrappy. The discomfort is the director's.

The second is the scene with the folk-rock group and the stampede for the discarded guitar. The scene has the mark of tourism on it, a phenomenon observed by an outsider and included for completeness' sake. Obviously Antonioni would not be a member of such a group in Italy any more than in England, but he would have known a thousand subtle things about Italian youths and their backgrounds that might have made them seem particularized, less a bunch of representatives *en bloc.*

The third questionable element is the use of the clown-faced masquers at the beginning and the end—which really means at the end, because they would not have been used at the start except to prepare for the end. Firstly, the texture of these scenes is jarring. Their symbolism—overt and conscious—conflicts with the digested symbolism of the rest of the film. It has a mark of strain and unfamiliarity about it, again like a phenomenon observed (partying Chelsea students, perhaps) and uncomfortably adapted. It is Cocteau strayed into Camus.

Much has been made of the clowns' thematic relevance, in that they provide a harbor of illusion for the hero after a fruitless voyage into reality. But precisely this thematic ground provides an even stronger objection to them, I think, than the textural one mentioned above. Thematically I think that the film is stronger without them, that it makes its points more forcibly. Suppose the picture began with Hemmings coming out of the flophouse with the derelicts, conversing with them, then leaving them and getting into his Rolls. At once it seems more like Antonioni. And suppose it ended (where in fact I thought it was going to end) with the long shot of Hemmings walking away after he has discovered that the corpse has been removed. Everything that the subsequent scene supplies would already be there by implication—*everything*—and we would be spared the cloudy symbols of high romance. Again it would be more like Antonioni.

All three of these lapses can possibly be traced to his working in a country where every last flicker of association and hint is not familiar and subconsciously secure.

On the other hand I think that two much-repeated criticisms of *Blow-up* are invalid. Some have said that Antonioni seemingly ridicules the superficial world of fashion but is really reveling in it, exploiting it. It is hard to see how he could have made a film on this subject without photographing it. One may as well say that, in exploring the world of sexual powers and confusions in *A Married Woman* Godard merely exploited nudity. By showing us the quasi-tarts of fashion (sex-appeal, instead of sex, by the hour) in all their gum-chewing vapidity and by showing us how easily the Super-Beautiful can be confected by someone who understands beauty, Antonioni does more than mock a conspicuously-consuming society: he creates a laughable reality against which to pose a genuinely troubling ambiguity.

Another widespread objection has been to the role that Vanessa Redgrave plays. The character has been called unclear. But this seems to me true only in conventional 19th-century terms of character development. In a television interview with me, Antonioni said that Miss Redgrave read the script and wanted to play the part because—he lifted his hand in a gesture of placement on the screen—"*Sta li.*"

"She stands there"; she has no explanations, no antecedents, no further consequences in the hero's life. I take this to mean that she is an analogue of the murder itself, an event rather than a person, unforgettable yet never knowable, and therefore perfectly consonant with the film.

Purely professionally from an actress's view, the role was a challenge because she has only two scenes, and those relatively brief appearances have to be charged with presence at once satisfying and tantalizing. Miss Redgrave met this challenge with ease, I think, not only because she has beauty and personality and distinctive talent but because she played the role against an unheard counterpoint: a secret and complete knowledge of who this young woman was. There was almost a hint that she was protecting Hemmings, that if he knew all that she knew, his life would disintegrate.

Thus my year of recurrent involvement with *Blow-up* and some observations about it. Now Antonioni has announced that he will make a film in America. I have two feelings about this. I am glad: because I would like to see how he sees America, just as I was glad to see his view of London. I also have reservations: because he functions more completely where he is rooted. Fine directors like Renoir and Duvivier and Seastrom and Eisenstein have all made films away from home, all of which contain good things but none of which is that man's best work. Some directors, like Lean and Huston, have functioned at their best in foreign places, but they are not quintessentially social directors. Antonioni (like Bergman in this respect) has been best in a society that is second nature to him, that has long fed and shaped him, that he has not had to "study."

It is a considerable miracle that he made *Blow-up* as well as he did. Its imperfections arise, I think, from having to concentrate on the miracle. Still, to say that I like *Blow-up* the least of his films since *L'Avventura* is a purely relative statement. I would be content to see one film a year as good as *Blow-up*—from Antonioni or anyone else— for the rest of my life.

Antonioni in Transit
by MARSHA KINDER

After *Red Desert* many people claimed that Antonioni had reached a dead end, that he was obsessed with the same theme in all his films and probably would never be able to break from its confined path. Then came *Blow-Up*, which seems to be a radical departure both in theme and technique. Yet upon closer examination, I think we can find that although *Blow-Up* may move in a new direction, the road it follows definitely leads from the earlier films. Perhaps the three most obvious differences are these. Antonioni no longer focuses on the inner life of his characters or on emotional relationships, but is primarily concerned with contemporary art. His central character is no longer Monica Vitti playing a sensitive, suffering female, but an energetic David Hemmings playing a successful photographer in tune with the modern scene. The place is no longer exceedingly slow with long lingering shots—but rapid, almost breathless.

The four films before *Blow-Up* (*L'Avventura*, 1959; *La Notte*, 1960; *L'Eclisse*, 1962; *Deserto Rosso*, 1964) do develop a single dominant theme—a sense of loss in the realm of motions and personal relationships. Antonioni was concerned with the emergence of a new kind of personal relationship, for which most people are unprepared emotionally because their education, upbringing and culture have aroused a set of expectations which are difficult to reject yet no longer fulfilled in a modern world dominated by business and science. I do not mean to suggest that Antonioni's attitude is simply a nostalgic longing for the 'good old days'; it's more complex than that. He does not imply that the new world is totally negative, but recognises it has many important values—the power necessary for man to master his environment; an efficiency which may improve his lot by wiping out hunger,

From Sight and Sound, *36 (Summer 1967): 132–37. Copyright © 1967 by the British Film Institute. Reprinted by permission of the author.*

78

poverty and physical pain; and the creation of a pure, abstract beauty. Yet despite these values, he also suggests that this world poses a real threat because it implies the loss of other values—of long-term personal relationships, of the uniqueness of the individual. Thus, he presents us with a clash between two incompatible value systems, which is essentially a tragic view.

Since Antonioni is primarily concerned with the influence of external conditions on the interior life of his characters, he had to use the right kind of character who could reveal these effects. His solution was to focus on a woman as the central character, and her relations with a less sensitive man. In an interview, he once said: "I think that reality can be filtered better through women's psychologies. They are more instinctive, more sincere." This sounds very much like Henry James's explanation of why he usually chose a woman for his centre of consciousness, and James was also concerned with an interior view. But perhaps a more important reason is that the woman is the one for whom the older values are most important; a stable love for husband and children is usually the centre of a woman's life. She is the one for whom the changes are most threatening, for she must find a completely new role in the new world. Moreover, the feminine principle is most closely identified with the values of the past that are being lost—sensitivity to human feeling, intuition, and instinctiveness. Once Antonioni shifted his focus of attention away from the interior life of his characters, he was no longer restricted to a female central character.

I do not mean to imply that the four films do not show any development: they definitely treat this main theme in different ways. For one thing, there is a growing recognition of and emphasis on the values of the new world: they are almost absent from *L'Avventura,* clearly present in *La Notte* and *L'Eclisse,* and receive considerable attention in *Red Desert.* Also, there are important differences in the central characters played by Monica Vitti. Claudia in *L'Avventura* begins naively with a belief in the old values, but painfully gains an understanding of the loss. Yet at the end she tries to maintain as much human contact as possible and settles for the limited relationship with Sandro in an attempt to compensate for the loss. In contrast, Valentina in *La Notte* knows about the loss from the beginning and is unwilling to settle for the limited relationship. Instead she remains emotionally detached yet longing for the impossible. Like Valentina, Vittoria in *L'Eclisse* also knows about the loss from the beginning, yet like Claudia she is willing to accept a limited relationship but without fooling herself that it is compensating for the loss. Although this gives her superior understanding and makes her the most stable and realistic of all the central characters, she does not have a capacity for feeling that is superior to Piero's as Claudia's was superior to Sandro's.

Giuliana of *Red Desert* also has the awareness of the loss from the beginning, but without the willingness to accept the limited relationship. In her case, the awareness leads to selfish narcissism and a psychological breakdown. She is struggling, not for awareness like Claudia, but for the ability to accept the new world—for some kind of reconciliation, which she finally achieves. Yet all of these characters would ideally like to have the same thing: either the old type of relationship, which is no longer possible, or complete emotional independence, which would enable them to live in the modern world without pain. That is what Vittoria means when she tells Piero, "I wish I didn't love you . . . or that I loved you more." It also explains Giuliana's contradictory fantasies of having either everyone who ever loved her to be around her like a wall, or the complete emotional freedom expressed in her story of the young girl alone on the island who is caressed by the sand, sea and rocks. Anna and Valentina actually strive for such independence.

Antonioni does not offer an easy answer to the problem of the conflict between the two value systems. He seems to accept the new world as inevitable although it means a sacrifice of important values from the past. The only hope seems to be understanding and a sympathetic acceptance of whatever human contact is possible. Understanding alone won't suffice—as Anna, Valentina and Giuliana demonstrate. Nor will an unthinking acceptance—as in the case of Sandro, Giovanni, Piero and Giuliana's husband. The most positive characters must achieve both, as Claudia and Vittoria ultimately do.

Although these four films focus on how changes in the modern world affect human relationships, they also imply that a similar change is taking place in art. For example, both central male characters in *L'Avventura* and *La Notte*—Sandro and Giovanni—are artists who sold out; and in both cases the loss in artistic power is linked to their failure in a love relationship. The change is also reflected in the examples of modern art that appear in the films—especially architecture. In *La Notte*, *L'Eclisse* and *Red Desert* there are many shots of huge modern buildings, obviously not built on human scale, which deflate the importance of the individual human being while celebrating the power of man's accomplishment. These buildings undeniably have beauty, yet of a particular kind—one that is clean, pure and abstract. For example, the huge radar towers in *Red Desert* are the products of science and technology, yet their design is lovely, delicate and graceful. They al-

"From the group of bums the face of the photographer detaches itself." (Clair)

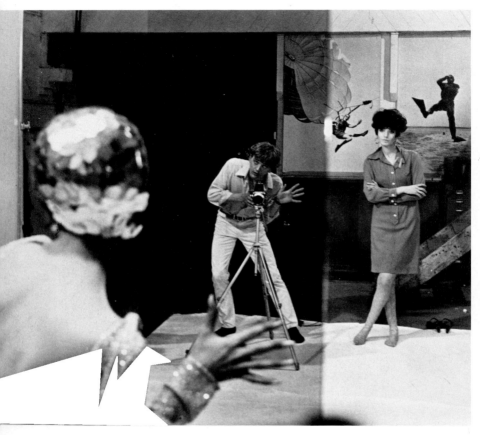

"Behind the partition of glass, reality seems to be in disorder."
(S. B.)

". . . the various kinds of distance separating artist and subject."
(Ross)

". . . interpreting ambiguous art
is like solving a mystery. . . ."
(Kinder)

". . . a custodian of the past refuses to sell. . . ." (Freccero)

" '. . . Of silly wood and senseless park;
and only in my heart the dark.' " (Kozloff)

". . . a spectacle of carnal Calvary." (Sarris)

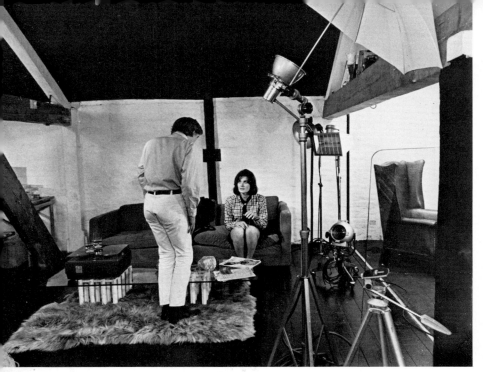

". . . the rhythm between friendship and estrangement. . . ."
(Slover)

"... the swamping of consciousness by the conduits of technology. ..." (Kauffmann)

" 'Death resides even in Arcady.' " (Freccero)

". . . a blow-up that transforms an idyll in a park into a scene of dread and terror." (Knight)

most look like huge geometric webs; but they make the men who are climbing them seem like little spiders, which helps to explain why they are so frightening to Giuliana. The most important point that Antonioni seems to stress is that individuals appear out of place in these buildings or imprisoned by their precise geometric patterns.

I think we can best examine the change in art and its relationship to the theme of emotional loss by focusing on *L'Avventura*. Sandro is an architect who gave up design in order to specialise in making financial estimates. His excuse for selling out is that buildings are no longer built for centuries, but are replaceable like people. The accuracy of this statement is supported by many shots in the film. For example, the opening scene shows modern apartment buildings encroaching on the villa of Anna's father; the villa is as outmoded as his conception of marriage. Later when Sandro and Claudia visit the deserted village, he calls the architecture 'madness.' The entire village has outlived its usefulness and is now like a skeleton or graveyard. It presumably was built for workmen on a job, but when the work was over the village no longer had any use. In the modern world, men go where the work is; they no longer have any roots. Other examples are the buildings being transformed from a means of personal expression or seclusion to a public institution. For example, the police headquarters at Milazzo was once a beautiful villa, a monument of art, a means of personal expression for the builder, who (someone observes) is probably turning over in his grave. Similarly, someone humorously suggests that Montaldo's villa be turned into an insane asylum.

The signs of change in art are not limited to architecture. The abstract, dehumanised quality comes out in the scene where Claudia visits the art gallery, while Anna and Sandro are making love. She is more intrigued and delighted by the reactions of the people than by the paintings, which have no relation to human beings. The lack of permanence is also suggested in the scene where they discover the ancient vase on the island. It has lasted for centuries, but as soon as someone from the modern world touches it, it is destroyed. There is also a suggestion that art has become a source of exploitation, a means to an end rather than an end in itself. For example, Goffredo uses his paintings merely to express his sexual desire and as a means of gratifying that desire by seducing his models. In their momentary passion he and Giulia knock over his easel and carelessly destroy the 'art.' Similarly, Gloria (the prostitute who takes Claudia's and Anna's place with Sandro) claims that she is a writer who communicates with the spirits of Tolstoi and Shakespeare. She reduces art to a cheap publicity trick and exploits it just as she exploits sex: she is a cheap substitute both for art and love. Thus, in this film Antonioni implies that art has undergone three main changes: it is no longer permanent, it is no longer related to human subjects or to the individual, and it has become a source of economic exploitation.

The implications of these changes are developed much further in *Blow-Up*. In this film contemporary art not only lacks permanence, but actually values the moment. This helps to explain why the central character is a photographer rather than an architect, for photography is concerned with capturing the moment. Moreover, contemporary art places a value on something in a particular context. One of the basic justifications of pop art, for example, is that it takes familiar objects and puts them into a new context that gives them a new value. In other words, the value lies not in the object itself, but in its relationship with a specific context. This notion is mocked in the scene where Thomas goes to hear the Yardbirds and gets away with part of the smashed guitar. The fragment, which was so highly valued in that particular situation, is merely a worthless piece of junk once he gets outside into a new context. The importance of context is also implied in his selection of the propeller at the antique shop. It is the one item among all those antiques that is linked with the contemporary world—with technology, with dynamic motion. Once he has it at home in a different context, his excitement is considerably abated.

Secondly, contemporary art not only is abstract and detached from human involvement, but it actually becomes a substitute for such involvements. This is brought out in the comic scene when shooting his model with his camera becomes a substitute for sexual intercourse. Although Thomas claims he would prefer to shoot pictures of real people rather than beautiful models, he shows no greater understanding of the human significance of these photographs. In fact, he uses exactly the same language to describe them that he uses for his fashion photos. When one of these photos leads to the discovery of a murder, he is concerned with it only as it relates to his art—he never thinks of calling the police, or of finding out the motive, or helping to capture the murderers. In fact, he finds that the larger he blows up the pictures and the more distorted and ambiguous they become, the greater variety of interpretation they allow, and this leads him to the discovery of the murder. Thus, interpreting ambiguous art is like solving a mystery, which is almost precisely what his friend Bill had said about his own abstract painting [Plate IV]. It is no accident that Patricia (Sarah Miles) points to the similarity between Bill's painting and Thomas's blow-up of the body. This leads to a valuing of ambiguity for its own sake.

Thirdly, the economic exploitation of art is practised not only by the amateur (like Goffredo) or the complete phoney (like Gloria), but by the most competent artists, which implies it has become an accepted part of contemporary art. The commercial photographer and the rock and roll star who are really 'good' are expected to succeed—to make money, to be well received. The stereotype of the artist is no longer an undiscovered genius starving in the garret. Artistic talent and success have become compatible and almost synonymous.

The expanded treatment of these changes leads to two other important implications about contemporary art. It implies that the creative process depends on accident and spontaneity and is really not carefully controlled. For example, Bill suggests that he is not sure of what he is doing while he is painting, that the creative process is marked by confusion; the control comes in after the painting is done and is manifested in the act of interpretation—of finding one little area that works. Similarly, Thomas takes many shots very rapidly and then goes through the careful process of selecting the one he will use. It is the act of interpreting the pictures taken in the park that arouses all the excitement. The value of spontaneity and accident is also apparent in the scene where the Yardbirds are performing before a passive audience, which suddenly is transformed into a screaming mob when one of the singers 'spontaneously' smashes his guitar. Whether the whole thing was planned and merely appeared spontaneous, is ambiguous; but in either case, spontaneity is clearly valued.

Another characteristic of contemporary art is the confusion between the artist (the creator) and his instrument of creation. This is another example of ambiguity and is linked to the minimising of control that the artist has during the act of creation. This idea is suggested in the mob's reaction to the guitar, and also in the relationship between Thomas and his camera. At one point he contradicts himself by saying he 'saw' the murder, when what he really means is that his camera saw it.

I do not mean to imply that *Blow-Up* is solely about art, but rather that it is the main focus. As in the earlier films, there is a very strong relationship between art and life—and it is not at all clear which imitates which. For example, the valuing of the moment is also suggested by Thomas's extremely short interest span in any subject, by the concern with fashionable clothes, by the conspicuous absence of any long-term relationships, and by the owner of the antique shop who is tired of old things. The detachment is reflected at the marijuana party, where everyone turns on and tunes out. It also is implied in the love triangle between Bill, Patricia and Thomas, which significantly never really develops. She wants to leave Bill and apparently is attracted to Thomas. When she comes to ask him for help, she realises it is useless.

There is a simultaneous conversation going on about her situation and the murder he has discovered. If he didn't bother to find out who was killed and why and by whom, then how can she possibly expect him to help her?

Ambiguity is perhaps the most obvious quality in the film. We find it in the dress of the people on the street, which makes it very difficult to tell the boys from the girls. We see it in Sarah Miles' dress, which purposely makes it ambiguous as to whether she is wearing anything underneath. We see it in the antique shop where the man's face is hidden behind the screen. Or in the scene where Thomas picks Jane (Vanessa Redgrave) out of a crowd. Or in the behaviour of the teen-agers, which is a baffling combination of extreme shyness and boldness. And perhaps most obviously, in the neon sign over the park, which Antonioni had constructed to be intentionally ambiguous and which is only momentarily in focus. Thus, as in his earlier films, Antonioni is suggesting that there is a new style of behaviour which is in marked contrast to a more traditional body of values, but his emphasis is on the changes in art rather than in human relationships.

The important question we should raise is how this shift in focus leads to differences in technique, for any good director uses the formal elements of his film to express the meaning. The answer is obvious with respect to colour; it is no longer used to reflect subjective views of reality and emotional attitudes as it was in *Red Desert*. But I think we can learn more about the changes in *Blow-Up* by focusing on this question with reference to pace and structure. In *Blow-Up* there is a radical change in pace as compared with the earlier films. The only similarity is that it has an important expressive function in both. The pace in the earlier films is generally very slow, and this has the signifi-cant function of taking the emphasis away from the action and focusing it instead on the mood or inner feelings of the characters. There are, for example, the long, lingering shots in *La Notte* of Lidia (Jeanne Moreau) wandering aimlessly at the party or through the streets. Nothing particular happens, but that is precisely the point; it is the slowness of pace that reveals her emotional state. These characters are all looking for something that is missing, but they are not sure what it is or where to find it. The visual images are charged with emotional effects that take time to work on the viewer.

The most effective use of pacing in the four films occurs in *L'Eclisse*, where it is absolutely essential to the film's meaning. The centre of interest is the relationship between Vittoria and Piero, who represent two worlds that move at entirely different speeds; and this difference in pace helps to define each world and its values. Vittoria is a translator and belongs to the world of the humanities; her world moves very slowly, for it is concerned with preserving the values of the past. When she is alone, she moves slowly and follows her interest and curiosity wherever they may lead her without worrying about the time. In contrast, Piero works at the Stock Exchange and belongs to the world of business and finance that moves at a frantic pace and focuses on the future. He never stands still for a moment and is always worried about wasting his time, for in this world time is money. The contrast in pace definitely controls their relationship. While he is eager to begin the affair, she is hesitant because she is aware of the inevitable result. Their relationship is like an eclipse, which implies two things. First, an eclipse suggests a loss, or a dimming of power; and their relationship is certainly limited. Secondly, an eclipse also implies a temporary period when the paths of two heavenly bodies are in conjunction. This is exactly what human relationships have become—brief moments of togetherness between longer periods of emotional isolation, the temporary conjunction of two human bodies moving in different orbits at different speeds. The difference in pace is an indication that their relationship cannot last.

Antonioni arranges the incidents in the film to heighten the contrast in pace. The two rapidly paced scenes in the stock market are preceded and followed by some of the slowest scenes in the film. Within the first scene at the stock market, there is a moment of silence that also works by the principle of contrast. The silence is a sign of respect for a dead colleague, a human relationship; yet he is only granted a minute. Moreover, this minute accentuates the excitement of the market's normal activity, just as the brief affair between Piero and Vittoria heightens the awareness of their normal state of isolation.

The rapid pace of *Blow-Up* is well suited to a character who is constantly on the move and concerned with capturing the moment. The pace of the film helps to express Thomas's conception of art and experience. He constantly moves from one context to another and is incapable of focusing his attention on a subject for very long, and this is partially expressed by the rapid succession of visual images. Not one single episode in the film is sustained; there are always interruptions. For example, in the scene between Jane and Thomas at his studio, their attention constantly shifts from their respective goals of getting back the film and finding out why she wants it, and is attracted by such things as the telephone, the music, smoking a cigarette, her posture. Finally, when they are about to make love—which represents a distraction for Jane, who carelessly throws aside the film that she was so desperately seeking—they are interrupted by the delivery boy bringing the propeller. Another example is the brilliant scene where Thomas is developing the photos taken in the park and reaching various interpretations, which are expressed almost entirely in visual terms. This is the point where Thomas is most engaged by any activity, yet it is also interrupted by a 'phone call and then by the hilarious encounter with the two teenagers. Thus, in this film as in *L'Eclisse,* the pace is essential to the meaning.

If we turn to the structure of *Blow-Up,* we find that it shares similarities with that of the earlier films, but they are used for different functions. The basic structure of all five films is a cyclical pattern comprised of episodes which contain a certain amount of repetition and leave a number of questions unanswered. One way of achieving the cyclical quality is by having every picture begin and end in the morning. In the earlier films the repetitious cycle implies the interchangeability of persons. For example, Claudia replaces the missing Anna in *L'Avventura.* We are never told why she left, but we discover the answer by focusing on Claudia. At the end of the film, Claudia is in Anna's position—she is aware of the limited nature of her relationship with Sandro and of his weakness, but instead of withdrawing like Anna she accepts it. Similarly, in *L'Eclisse* we don't have to see the ending of Vittoria's affair with Piero because we have already seen the break with Riccardo, and presumably it will be just the same. The absence of a conventional dramatic structure also helps to suggest that in these films action is not the main focus and that the central meaning must be found elsewhere.

This is not at all the case in *Blow-Up.* Here, the absence of a conventional dramatic plot and the unanswered questions help to reveal Thomas's fragmented view of experience, which is comprised of separate moments. No episode reaches a climax or resolution; no human relationship builds or develops. This structure also implies that Thomas doesn't really care about finding the answers. In *L'Avventura* Claudia at first thought she cared about what happened to Anna, then only pretended to care, and finally had to admit she really didn't and to accept what that implied. But in *Blow-Up* there is no pretence: motives, causes, people simply don't matter to Thomas. This lack of a conventional plot also helps to express Thomas's conception of art. If an artist assumes that accident and spontaneity play an important role in art and if he values ambiguity, then he is unlikely to have a tightly controlled plot with a resolution that neatly ties together all the loose ends; for such a structure implies that the artist has carefully planned out everything in advance. He avoids the conventional mystery plot.

Yet there is an irony in the structure of *Blow-Up.* Although on first view it seems to be episodic and rather random in order, a closer examination reveals that it does have a rather artificial order. Many of the encounters that Thomas has in the first half of the film (before he meets Jane) are repeated in reverse order in the second half, which makes a neat circular pattern after all. For example, it begins and ends in a morning when Thomas encounters the mime troupe. His next encounter is with the model whom he photographs, and whom he meets again at the party before going to look for the body the next morning. Next, he shoots the grotesque models, whom he refers to as 'birds' and whom he sneaks out on and leaves waiting with their eyes closed; which is paralleled by the scene right before the party where he hears the Yardbirds and their glassy-eyed audience and manages to sneak out with the piece of guitar. After leaving the models, he goes next door to see Bill and his girl friend, a visit which he repeats before the scene with the Yardbirds. Returning from his first visit, he runs into the two teenage girls, who show up later while he is developing the photos before he makes his second visit to Bill. The two central episodes are his two major encounters with Jane—the first meeting in the park is framed by two visits to the antique shop, and the second encounter in his studio is preceded by his stop in the restaurant and terminated by the arrival of the propeller from the antique shop, which links it to the first meeting. The structure, then, is not haphazard, which implies a distance between Thomas's and Antonioni's view of art. I think this distinction can be clarified by a closer examination of the mime troupe, which frames the film.

The art of the mime troupe in the final scene suggests an important contrast with the other examples of art in the film. For one thing, it is not temporary; pantomime is a traditional art form linked to the past, and the imaginary tennis game is a sustained creation that does build. Secondly, it is an art which requires engagement—not only from the performers, but also from the audience looking on who contribute to the illusion. It also requires the involvement of the camera, which follows the path of the imaginary ball; and finally succeeds in winning the active participation of Thomas, who has been detached throughout the film. He actually retrieves the imaginary ball for them, and has to put down his camera to do it. This act recalls the first interaction between Thomas and the troupe in the opening scene when he contributes money to their cause. Thirdly, the artists in this instance are in control of what they are creating: the illusion of the spontaneous or accidental (that is, when the ball goes over the fence) is obviously controlled; there is no instrument (like a guitar or camera) other than the creators themselves; the ambiguity between illusion and reality is carefully controlled and is based upon a wilful act of imagination that is totally missing from Thomas's conception of art. This is the kind of art that is being replaced in the contemporary world, and its position at the end of the film helps to stress its significance.

I am suggesting, then, that Antonioni is critical of the style he employs in *Blow-Up*. It is not that the style is inherently 'bad,' but that it can be used to imply a conception of experience that threatens to destroy values of the past. Yet he demonstrates that he can use it as effectively as his contemporaries. In this film he seems to allude to the styles of others, which was not characteristic of his earlier films—the fast pace of Lester, the Hitchcock-like treatment of the murder in the park, the mime troupe which seems to belong in a Fellini film, and even the allusiveness which is so characteristic of Godard. Yet he uses the allusions quite differently by making the borrowed elements peculiarly his own, by making them essential to the meaning of his own film, by putting them in a new context while still retaining and exploiting the context from which they are derived. This is the essence of artistic control, which is so antithetical to Thomas's conception.

Although Antonioni sacrifices the inner exploration of character, which was one of his greatest accomplishments in his earlier films, he does so intentionally in order to achieve a different focus and to develop different implications of his dominant theme. He could not have done so without altering his style.

BLOW-UP:
Antonioni and the Mod World
by JAMES F. SCOTT

On first viewing, *Blow-Up* seems too clever, just too clever. How can anyone be so coy with a camera without losing himself in visual display? From the film's opening moment, when splinters of dramatic action burst through the titles until David Hemmings is erased from the last scene by a trick of the optical printer, Michelangelo Antonioni never relaxes his insistence upon striking effects. Shots through layers of glass, props to complicate composition, splashes of expressionistic red, deep-focus and wide-angle fixes that draw the eye to incidental detail: the photography never ceases to dazzle. And yet I am now convinced this picture is much more than the cinematic equivalent of a Mary Quant dress. The mad mod world of London has found its poet, but has not found him in exactly a celebratory mood. Antonioni's highly complex reaction to contemporary English culture creates the thematic core of what must surely rank among the finest films of the sixties.

However brief his residence in London, the Italian director already knows this world well, its pace, its idiom, its style. He is not just the enthralled tourist, gawking at mini skirts and pink tights, even though such gear provides much of the surface phenomena of the film. As always, his bent is analytical and documentary, his attention devoted to the psychology underlying gesture and speech. His unnamed protagonist (played with supreme cool by Hemmings) might have been lifted from one of the Beatle records, for, like the musical hero fashioned by John Lennon, he's "a real Nowhere Man . . ." who "doesn't have a point of view/Knows not where he's going to." But in An-

From Cross Currents *(Spring 1967): 227–33. Copyright © 1967 by Cross Currents. Reprinted by permission of the author.*

tonioni the lyricism of the Beatles gives way to more ambiguous tonalities which, in spite of occasional dissonance, are arranged with great care, almost cunning. Down to the last stroke of the imaginary tennis game at its close, *Blow-Up* is the work of a virtuoso. At the same time, though, it is a telling commentary upon the psychic defenses of man, particularly the man of artistic temper. Antonioni's seriousness about these matters reclaims the film, even when it comes close to triteness and sensationalism.

Paradoxically, this is perhaps Antonioni's most personal film. Like Bergman's *The Magician* and Fellini's *8½*, it is another version of "a portrait of the artist," here a commercial photographer. Of course, Antonioni avoids the confessional. The young man with the camera is no more the director himself than Herr Vogler, the traveling magician who does tricks with a magic lantern, is really Ingmar Bergman. But Antonioni surely feels the force of professional cousinship to his hero. Like the director who created him, the protagonist of *Blow-Up* is intelligent, aloof, objective, technically expert, sometimes exploitative, and even a little worried about his obligations toward those who get into the view finder of his camera. He knows the strain of urban isolation but sees no relief from it; "I'm off London this week," he confides to a buddy, but these efforts at escape are no more significant than the chatter of the girl in the secondhand shop about emigrating to Nepal. He also senses, at least vaguely, the ambiguous position of an artist working with mass media. Critical of the public taste that furnishes his livelihood, he must devote himself to representing the life of a community whose values mean almost nothing to him. Does aesthetic detachment require a purely spectatorial attitude? Does art do nothing more than freeze a moment of experience with a snap of the shutter or a stroke of the brush? These questions, arising naturally from the plight of the protagonist, are really Antonioni's own. Though the director never gets so close as to be unable to judge his hero, the verdict is delivered against a kindred spirit.

In characterizing the artist-hero, the film summons up polarities we have all grown familiar with—art and life, illusion and reality, style and impulse. Those who wish Keats had turned his back on the Grecian urn and Yeats had stayed clear of Byzantium will immediately be put off by this. Yet Antonioni is rarely cliché, though he crosses few philosophical thresholds. His fable is carefully built, and his characters, even when they resemble zombies, seem fully real. If the meaning expands into allegory, its generalized significance emerges from an ensemble of concrete sights, sounds, and gestures. The task he sets for himself as a film-maker is to "defend the principle of intelligence within the heart of the real" (*Bianco e Nero,* 1958). This scrupulous fidelity to the sensate world enables him in *Blow-Up* both to assert the autonomy of art and measure the artist himself in moral terms.

To Antonioni, autonomy suggests distance, not escape, from life. But distance is crucial, because art imposes its claims indirectly; it does not have "meaning" in the ordinary journalistic sense. Bill the painter, Hemmings' closest associate, says of his own canvases: "They don't mean anything when I do them. Just a mess. Afterwards it sorts itself out—like a clue in a detective story." This echoes a remark Antonioni once made about his own work: "It can happen that films acquire meanings, that is to say, the meanings appear afterwards . . ." (*Positif*, 1959). Whether or not this parallel is significant, Bill's way of looking at his paintings provides a verbal paradigm for the plot of *Blow-Up*. Only by letting the meaning "sort itself out" does Hemmings discover the real subject of his photography. This, however, complicates the prospect of action based on artistic insight.

The revelatory possibilities of art, Antonioni implies, spring from the openness and curiosity of the artist. Hemmings plays the part of a good-natured vagabond, exceptionally sensitive to light and shape, with fingers that move over *F*-stops as smoothly as if he were performing on harp or violin. In the critical scene in the park, he comes upon the lovers just accidentally, while collecting some landscape shots to balance the somber tone of a volume of photographs. The unexpectedness of the lovers' presence is emphasized in the way Antonioni shoots the scene, the film camera first catching them as a colorful off-center blur in a few frames of a fast pan. As Hemmings first begins to pursue them, he has (beyond some voyeuristic interest) only an expectation that they will ornament the landscape more attractively than the pigeons whom they replace as his subjects. Even after his altercation with Vanessa Redgrave (like Hemmings, nameless in the film), the photographer still has no idea he has taken a picture of a murder. The point is simple, but well made. The real subject of art is distinct from the conscious designs of the artist, to which it often does violence. A qualifying note is added upon Hemmings' return to his studio: though art, like science, makes gains from serendipity, chance favors only the properly disposed.

Hemmings is thus favored because he is, whatever else, a fine photographer. Sensitive to composition, he notices the eccentricity of his subject's sight-line. Attentive to light, he sees a shadow he can't account for. He misarranges, then corrects, the sequence of shots, entertaining and later rejecting the hypothesis that Miss Redgrave is looking at him. From these notes a syndrome of details falls into place, for association and implication are the substance of artistic insight. During these moments as the prints are hung on the studio wall, the sound track effectively reinforces an imaginative reconstruction of reality, Hemmings' absorption in the world he has caught with his camera. While his concentration intensifies, the sound of wind stirs through the trees, and the clouds of that fatal twilight seem to re-gather. Now, too, we understand why Antonioni has made his protagonist specialize in black and white photography. Returning to the scene in the park, we go back to a world drained of color, an unreal-istic, self-evidently artificial world, yet one whose tones are more real than reality. Only when the park episode is printed out in black and white does the atmosphere seem sinister enough for murder. The film stock itself serves to unmask the picturesque. Moreover, in this special world of art, a meaningless, unfocused shadow gradually becomes a form, a man, a killer. The parable is now complete. When Bill's mistress later remarks that one of the blow-ups looks "just like one of Bill's paintings," she just underscores verbally what the action has already shown.

Art fixates, transforms, enlarges, and in so doing shows us aspects of reality we could never see with an unguided eye. I discern in this a special message from Antonioni to his critics, those who have looked askance at the seemingly arbitrary imagery in some of his earlier films. Watch closely, gentlemen; trifles are not always a trifling matter. Beyond this, however, there is the more obvious public meaning, central to *Blow-Up*. Art confers upon man a special kind of insight, yet not through magic or mystification, but through patience, crafts-manship, and mental alertness within an organized discipline.

Though if art is distinct from magic, this doesn't prevent its seem-ing magical to the uninitiate, or keep the artist himself from donning the robes of a mage. After all, the artist is a maker, and appears to create *ex nihilo*. There is something terribly beguiling about his office, which makes it a source of power. And that is why, I think, Antonioni's hero finds his profession so attractive. He is a weak man, rootless and confused, who uses his camera for ego support.

Camera in hand or in reach, the hero is sturdy and stylish. He can control his environment, choosing the roles he will play (worker, lover) and the terms on which he will play them (the escape clause of professional distance). This is not necessarily bad, of course, for every artist counterfeits those roles which extend an opportunity to create. The problem with Antonioni's protagonist is that behind the mask there seems to be no face. Personalities fall off him as readily as the roving picket's "Ban the Bomb" sign tumbles from the rear seat of his automobile. He needs the camera to maintain his identity, for without it he is quickly caught up and lost in every crowd that gathers. At the mercy of his surroundings, his private self is too weak to withstand the world. Antonioni's interest in the camera as a power surrogate thus governs the argument of the film, offering the chief clue to the judgment he passes upon the central character.

The talismanic authority of the camera is nowhere more evident than when it is used as a sexual instrument, as in the sequence where Hemmings is first shown photographing a model. Much more than an isolated extravagance, this episode establishes a pattern running through all the scenes in which he exhibits strength. His camera, its threats and its promises, confers upon him a mastery over his associates. On this occasion, he feigns the role of lover, and with absolute success. His relationship with the model is purely professional, yet Antonioni composes the scene so as to make their encounter simulate sexual climax, complete with verbal enticements, erotic movement, gradual convergence, and eventual exhaustion. The clicking shutter of the camera marks the rhythm of this engagement, underscoring the importance Antonioni attaches to the visible badge of his hero's profession.

Having established this motif in a single scene, Antonioni now extends and complicates it, as Hemmings uses his camera to control the reactions of a wide range of persons—the sophisticated manikins of his studio, a desperate Vanessa Redgrave, and the absurd teen-agers who stumble into his path. For the painted creatures of the studio, the photographer's authority is absolute, whatever mockery and contempt is implicit in the way it is exercised. As for the girls who come calling after hours, they epitomize the same subservience at a comic level—the fantasy of male power associated with the camera. The mere promise of an eventual chance to model brings them stumbling out of their clothes in order to be sexually available to their benefactor. Flopping about like bewildered seals in an ocean of purple paper, these outrageously inept coquettes bring to grotesque summation the theme of ego-support derived from professional status.

As might be expected, the relationship between Hemmings and Miss Redgrave is more complex, exhibiting both the strength and weakness of the protagonist. While he plays the role of artist, his personal power is again reinforced by his camera. In the park, when Miss Redgrave protests his invasion of her privacy, he brushes her objections aside with brash clinical detachment: "It's not my fault if there's no privacy in the world." Apparently he has declared perpetual open season upon those who get in front of his camera. And he is still fully in command when she comes to the studio to plead for the incriminating film. So long as he holds it, he can have her as mistress or model, even restyle her personality according to his specifications and make a game of her incompetent efforts to steal the camera. The relationship changes, however, the moment he becomes personally implicated in her affairs. Suspecting nothing in her private life beyond a conventional liaison with an older man, he is shocked to find her connected with a murder plot. The discovery in the photo lab jars him completely out of the studied, easy composure he has turned into a rule of life. He loses his cool. Ironically, the honesty of his art explodes the artifice of his personal style, by forcing his attention upon a disturbing existential fact.

Significantly, in the scenes that follow his leaving the studio, he is without his camera. He can no longer control his environment. Alone, he is nervous and frightened. In crowds, he is immediately stamped with the collective image. Fumbling about the darkened streets of London, he is quite another person than the man who orders around the mascara-bedecked minions of his studio.

Look at the difference, for example, between the two scenes in the park, first when he is protected by his camera, then when he goes back to search for the corpse. Trailing the lovers, he was poised, self-assured, moving so bouncily as almost to dance. Returning to the scene, he is jittery, faltering, upset by incidental noises of the night, obsessed by a confused plan to "get help." His white garb against the deep green backdrop gives him something close to a spectral appearance. Should the police be telephoned? Apparently not before this impulse receives positive support from his friends.

Like nearly all Antonioni's heroes, Hemmings evades his spiritual crises with a benumbing emotional binge. First it's the Yardbirds' concert, which he blunders into but can't seem to leave. The audience, fixed in hypnotic stupor, traps him with its inertia, forcing him to listen to the adolescent vocalist who thumps out, ironically, a song about "goin' on." So close is Hemmings' inadvertent identification with this quivering glob that when he finally escapes during a moment of riot, he comes away with a sizeable hunk of a dismembered guitar. If this is the fruit of accident, his deliberate devices are still more disastrous. While the teen-agers go on jazz jags, their elders get high on pot. In the temple of narcotic euphoria he now visits, conscious life has collapsed altogether. "I thought you were going to Paris," he tells one of the guests. "This is Paris," she rejoins. The keynote of the scene is struck as the camera briefly lingers upon a volume of Van Gogh's paintings; madness and self-destructive brutality rule this world, though it lacks the redeeming assertiveness of Van Gogh. In the hell of Sartre's *No Exit,* the damned eternally confront one another with lidless eyes. But the marijuana enthusiasts are fully protected against this mark of existential awareness: their eyelids are permanently rolled down into a visionless squint. Quickly enervated by this atmosphere, the protagonist himself settles down into unconsciousness.

"After such knowledge, what forgiveness?" Antonioni might well repeat T. S. Eliot's question. Confronted by the nasty reality of violent death, Hemmings is totally incapacitated. It's not that he should have played the hard-boiled private-eye, hunting down the guilty woman like some latter-day Bogart. What she's guilty of remains less than clear, perhaps active involvement, perhaps only accidental complicity. All we really know of the heroine comes from her own lips ("my private life is very confused"), hardly sufficient evidence for conviction. In any event, Antonioni isn't interested in pressing an accessory-after-the-fact charge against his hero. The focus of concern is this man's complete inability to cope with a violation of the world he has worked so patiently to make secure. His remedy for disturbance is distraction—sex, song, drink, drugs. In the morning he will have second thoughts, but by morning the chance to act will have vanished forever. This is why Antonioni's films so often end in the morning, not just *The Red Desert,* but *The Adventure* and *The Night* as well. Missed opportunities seem most poignant as one carries an emotional hangover into a new, but unpromising, day.

In *Blow-Up,* however, the conclusion is protracted to considerable length, allowing time for the now famous (or notorious) tennis match which white-faced revellers play with an imaginary ball. Giving up his sleuthing, Hemmings is ready to play too, as is evident from his willingness to chase a stray shot and return the ball to the court. But who are the players and what's the score? It's tempting to take this scene as summarizing the motifs of escape and evasion that permeate the entire dramatic texture. Their grease-paint associates these bizarre performers with the strangely tinted models of the studio; their collective hallucination brings to mind both the jazz concert and the marijuana party; their enthusiasm for racing around in an automobile resembles the nervous exuberance of Hemmings himself behind the wheel. Opening and closing the film, their antics seem to frame and evaluate everything in between. In accepting their game, the protagonist might be said to embrace a regressive fantasy-life which permanently corrupts his being. But maybe not. While perfectly plausible, this reading strikes me as overly simple.

Whether by intention or accident, Antonioni has left the last scene of *Blow-Up* somewhat cryptic. I don't think he has quite made up his mind about the mods, or at least isn't ready to damn them *en masse.* One thing these youths have in their favor is their dissociation from the values of the past, which Antonioni so passionately rejected in a statement apropos of *The Adventure*:

We make use of an aging morality, of outworn myths, of ancient conventions. And we do this in full consciousness of what we are doing. Why do we respect such a morality?

He resents fiercely that man "is impelled by moral forces and myths which were already old in the time of Homer" and that "in the realm of the emotions, a total conformity reigns." However irresponsible, the mods have escaped the burden of these inhibitions. Antonioni was of two minds when he talked about them in the *Life* interview of January, 1966:

The young people among whom my film is situated are all aimless, without any other drive but to reach that aimless freedom. Freedom that for them means marijuana, sexual perversion, anything. . . .

Yet, on the other hand:

To live as a "swinger" . . . I think it means to take a leave from certain norms, certain traditions at any cost. . . . But maybe it's also a legitimate way to get near a happier condition of life. Who can tell?

This mixture of feelings enters into the last scene of *Blow-Up*.

The revellers, after all, are a little different from the marijuana crowd. We first see them collecting for charity, which may help no one, but seems well intentioned. They also appear to be really in touch with each other, not just rubbing shoulders while each pursues his private dream. Their eyes focus, too, if only on imaginary tennis balls. Though deliberately feigning, they apparently understand the difference between illusion and reality. Perhaps their posturing is an evasion of life, but it seems more like strategic retreat than unconditional surrender. We might make the same case for the artist-hero. He does not grow, but neither does he shrivel. In fact, the tennis match—repeating a game he watched before photographing the murder—seems to return him to an earlier stage of his life. He has recovered his style, his manner, and perhaps acquired some insight into his inclination to indulge in posturing. At least this is a matter for further critical debate.

Blow-Up is such an ocular *tour de force* it is hard to avoid being either aggravated or overwhelmed by it. Balanced appraisal, however, must take account of both fault and achievement. To me, the defects seem minor, but they are there. I am still not sure, for example, why Miss Redgrave doesn't simply expose the film during the moment she has the camera in her possession. And why is the nude scene with the would-be models drawn out so lengthily, particularly since Antonioni has to bundle the characters in paper wrappers to get them past the vice squad? Yet the total effect of the picture is one of expert finesse. Appropriate nuances are everywhere, and little snips of footage speak with quiet eloquence. Take, for instance, some of the paraphernalia associated with the protagonist. An ornamental propeller—ready to twirl endlessly without moving anything anywhere. Or the drawing of an Arabian caravan—stylishly parading across an empty wall of the studio. Or a bust of Louis XV—remembered by history for a single phrase, *"apres moi, le deluge."* Antonioni refuses to caress these objects with the affection of a symbol-monger. But how right they are, how fully relevant. The acting, too, is smooth, natural, while the composition and coloration will likely be studied by film technicians for the next decade.

The intellectual import of *Blow-Up* is more difficult to assess. Like his protagonist, Antonioni seems to resent any encroachment upon his moral neutrality. Critics who insist upon social consciousness as a *sine qua non* will probably regret that the director gives so little attention to his hero's connection with the world of the doss house. An orthodox Marxist might easily have built this moment of hesitant contact with the proletariat into an elaborate statement upon the parasitism of bourgeois art. On the other hand, those who seek from this picture some "spirituality" of a kind usually associated with pulpits will come away frustrated. Antonioni debunks Hugh Hefner, but not from the perspective of either Talcott Parsons or Cardinal Ottaviani. Perhaps there is no controlling perspective in the film, which gives some force to the charge of evasion. It might be argued, surely, that the neat paradox of the tennis match offers theatrical finality in place of human judgment.

My personal sympathies, however, lie with Antonioni. I don't like *Blow-Up* quite so much as *The Eclipse* or *The Red Desert,* but nothing in this film effaces my respect for the director's integrity, intelligence, and severe moral astringency. Rightly, he suspects both private mystiques and public orthodoxies. Of course, he merely sees *through,* never sees *to.* His visual rhetoric always shatters, never saves. At the end of *The Red Desert,* Giuliana tells her young son that the bird protects himself from sulfuric factory-smoke by learning to fly around it. At the human level, unfortunately, the problem is more complicated. I doubt that we will avoid the threats to our own survival by playing tennis in a London park, and gather that Antonioni doubts it too. But if anyone knows what we should be doing instead I wish he'd drop me a line.

Cool Times
by T. J. ROSS

The young celebrity-hero of *Blow-Up,* a film concerned with, among other things, the pandering to celebrity and consequent chic freakiness of London in the sixties, is played by David Hemmings, himself an actor who made it in the sixties mainly through playing representative youth roles. And Hemmings' function in the film is indeed to behave more as a representative type than to act as a discrete person. This follows, in part, from Antonioni's developing interest, most in force in his two latest films, *Blow-Up* and *Zabriskie Point,* in de-mythicizing the concept of personality (that is, of personality considered in its usual meaning of a fixed identity or pristine "individuality"). The star fashion photographer portrayed by Hemmings remains the most anonymous and protean of Antonioni's protagonists (as well as, it should be noted from the start, the most successful: he is neither a professional man "blocked" in his work and career like most of the male leads, nor, like the lead of *Il Grido,* a suicide). The abstract characterization also lends itself to a focus on the same ideas posed by Julio Cortázar in the short story that provided the film's title and point of departure: the problematic equation between an author and his hero, between a narrative and its embodying voice.

Cortázar begins his story:

> It'll never be known how this has to be told, in the first person or in the second, using the third person plural or continually inventing modes . . .[1]

Yet, ". . . one of us all has to write, if this is going to be told." As the story builds, with Cortázar (in his own voice) taking turns in the

[1] Julio Cortázar, *Blow-Up and Other Stories* (New York: Collier Books, 1968), p. 100.

telling with his narrator-hero Michel, indecisiveness about an estab-
lishing point of view becomes precisely the point. Michel's own point
of view is defined—and criticized—by the other voice as being too
literary:

> Michel is guilty of making literature, of indulging in fabricated un-
> realities. Nothing pleases him more than to imagine exceptions to
> the rule, individuals outside the species, not-always-repugnant mon-
> sters.[2]

Here, being literary is equated with being romantic. Throughout the
story, the other narrator interrupts to qualify or to confuse Michel's
more romantic interpretations of the relationship of a middle-aged
woman, a youth, and a third person seemingly waiting at a distance—
all beheld in a park. Nor are the shifting planes of narration merged
into a single unity of perspective or slant; rather, they take form only
as a mosaic of interpretive possibilities.

Antonioni shares Cortázar's dry, relentlessly quizzical manner. Like
Cortázar, he discourages in his audience any simple identification with
his lead figures; even as he discourages our impulse to define his own
attitudes and characteristics as those of his characters. *Blow-Up* certainly does not present a hero quickly identified with; yet in line with
the approach in Cortázar's story, in none of Antonioni's films is there
a more open play on the relationship between an *auteur* and his
persona; and in none are certain equations between the sensibility of
the creator and his creature more manifest.

In the story, Michel is an amateur photographer living in Paris;
Thomas, his counterpart in the film, is a professional photographer
living in London. The generation consciousness of the film, however,
matters far more than the geographical change; indeed, *Blow-Up* falls
into the current cycle of youth films through its categorical emphasis
on its hero's youth—an emphasis absent from the story (as are most
of the incidents of the film, including the culminating one at the
tennis court).

The transforming of its young protagonist into a youth-figure, then,
becomes a main departure from the story. By reason of his age alone,
Thomas is granted the prerogative of enjoying a freedom from the
neuroses that weigh down those heroes of other films who belong to
an earlier generation: by itself, this freedom would serve to bring him
closer to the awareness of the film-maker for whom the very process
of delineating the psychological blocks and dilemmas of the characters

[2] *Ibid.,* pp. 108–109.

of such films as *La Notte* or *L'Avventura* would seem to have been the means of moving beyond them. And, unlike the unidimensional young stockbroker played by Alain Delon in *L'Eclisse,* Hemmings' scene is one of art and fashion. In his kind of work, therefore, he comes closest to Antonioni's own *métier* than do any other of Antonioni's main characters. This introduces a third level of interest—in addition to those of youth-figure and authorial voice—in the presentation of the hero; for, in his presentation, we also find various hints of that old warhorse—and key mythological hero of Antonioni's own generation—the artist-figure. All of which brings us quite a long way from Cortázar's story. Again, in contrast to the story, the action of the film leads to a merging of viewpoints and consequent difference in thematic development in the final tennis court sequence—the tennis court itself reminding one, on the biographical level, of Antonioni's own youthful times as a tournament-winning tennis player. In sum, the progress of the Hemmings character through Chelsea-Knights-bridge-Hampstead embodies the related themes of youth and art.

Throughout the film, the focus is on Hemmings: what he represents —in the terms suggested—marks the key interest and is reinforced through the relative lack of documentary or atmospheric emphasis on London itself. The camera never pauses long enough to allow us to enjoy a shot of an historical site or other familiar locale. Unlike the quick Cook's tour along King's Road, for example, which Joseph Losey offers us in the opening shots of *The Servant,* Antonioni hardly gives us time to get our bearings. Nor does he present his characters as distinctively "British types" seen from a special or foreign point of view—no more than the characters of *Zabriskie Point* interest him as national types (a point lost on the film's numerous critics on this side of the Atlantic who bemoaned the unreality of its lead figures as— what Antonioni obviously was not, after all, aiming at—hippies on the all-American model).

II

We first see Hemmings stalking and "shooting" vagrants and other derelict figures of the streets; he has been commissioned to compile a series of photographic studies of such figures to be included in an expensively planned picture book on London, with special attention paid to its lower depths. The pictures must also serve to bring the volume to an upbeat close; so Hemmings is on the lookout too for people in poses suggestive of—in his editor's words—"peace and harmony," rather than outrage and violation. What better than shots of a couple strolling in a park seemingly on a lovers' amble? When developed and blown up, however, this last set of shots reveals that, what from his distance had appeared to be spontaneously playful and cajoling gestures on the part of the woman (Vanessa Redgrave) in the picture, had more likely been a series of calculated maneuvers culminating in that ultimate violation: murder. In a corner of one of the blow-ups is what looks like the body of her victim, hunched nervelessly on the ground in a pose similar to that of the derelicts hunched over in the street and "shot," by Hemmings earlier in the day.

"Peace" is precisely what is nowhere evident on our hero's rounds. When, in concern over the matter of his blow-ups, he seeks the editor of his book, the latter is shown finding his peace in pot; in his cloud of smoke, he remains impenetrable to Hemmings' queries. In a subsequent scene, when the woman in the park traces the photographer to his studio to plead for the return of the possibly incriminating photographs, she says in reaction to his sharp refusal: "You wouldn't act like this if these were times of peace!" To which he replies at once: "It's not my fault that there is no peace." She then offers to bed down with him as a means of getting her way, their exchange maintaining its curious equilibrium as, in the ensuing silence, he matches her sudden removal of her blouse by removing his shirt. An interruption at his door, however, draws him away, leaving the woman enough time to grab the pictures and run off.

The impromptu and abortive nature of this encounter is typical of all the other relationships depicted, whether personal or professional; it would seem to be typical of a time without peace. And the cool manner of all the characters—their manner is both unflappable and abrupt; both candid and aloof—is part of a style that clearly marks an adaptation to the jolting discontinuities of their experience. The discontinuous, unharmonious pace of things is also reflected in the varying degrees and kinds of sexual involvements pictured—none of which, to put it mildly, is on an idyllic plane.

The first of such scenes is that of the artist posing and photographing his model. As the phallic muzzle of his camera nudges toward the girl, who lies prone before it, Hemmings caresses her with his voice: ". . . better . . . better . . . easy . . . good . . . ah! . . . that's it . . . come on now . . . come . . . on . . ."; and she, in turn, is shown responding with more and more warmth to his directions. When his pictures have been taken, Hemmings abruptly stalks off, leaving his aroused model stretched out on the studio floor.

As a cogent, if gross, variation on a traditional theme of paintings devoted to the artist at work in his studio, this sequence is reminiscent of the various kinds of distance separating artist and subject, particularly the distance created by the inescapable conflict between their motives and expectations [Plate II]. We are led to recall Vermeer or Velasquez, especially the former's "The Artist's Studio," as Hemmings is shown with his back to the camera and in close shot, while his model is seen from over his shoulder, front face, and in medium distance. Like the painting, this shot captures the model in her reverie before the artist in his "inhuman" intentness. And for all the grunted admonishings and heavy breathings, the whole scene is dominated by a silence as deep and essential as Vermeer's.

Unlike his single sitter, the group of models with whom Hemmings is next shown at work is pictured more ruthlessly—caught by Antonioni's camera in a hard focus that brings out all that is callow, characterless, and stupid in their features. One good look is enough to propel us into a complicity of feeling—in a shared contempt for this team—with Hemmings. Three subjectivities—those of director, protagonist, and audience—are in this instance merged in recoil (even as we are brought willy nilly into sympathy with the heroines of such films as *La Notte* or *Red Desert* through the undeniable ungainliness and possible maleficence of what they are surrounded by, despite much about these heroines that might otherwise hold us to an objective or puzzled response). Here, we are led directly to the artist's viewpoint, for Hemmings' indifference to his models' feelings no doubt takes its inspiration from Antonioni's own coolness—as notorious as Hitchcock's—toward performers. By noting what is characteristic—indeed predictable—of Antonioni in this shot, we may qualify the more severely moralistic-Marxist criticisms that have been levelled at the film. A French film scholar, Annie Goldman, for example, has written that the power over and disdain for the models shown by the photographer is meant to be understood by the audience as "scandalous." Concerning the models themselves, Mrs. Goldman well points to ". . . the absence of all erotic value in these women whose skinniness is akin to the rigidity of dead bodies and whose pale makeup is responsible for their loss of individuality." [3] But where are we given the cue to blame the photographer for the models' grim preening and deathly self-distortions? They are simply his given materials. What is clear in the contrast between his manner with them and his more benign and sociable response to the group of clownish revellers—their faces also painted—in whose games he joins at the film's end. Before this moment, however, we first note several other games, including the sexual, that we see him—with varying degrees of constraint—drawn into.

[3] Annie Goldman, "On *Blow-Up*," *Tri Quarterly*, Winter, 1968, p. 64.

Like the game he is led to play with his fans—who barge in on him in the person of two teen-age girls. This sequence of the artist and his fans serves as a complement to those of the artist and his models. It, too, takes place in silence, for even as the girls literally tear at the photographer, they are unable to express what exactly they want from him. Fatter than the models and more directly grasping, they prove equally grotesque. Half to show his contempt, and half in bemused self-defense, Hemmings responds by tearing at their clothes, until all three begin wrestling in an orgiastic play determined by impulses which appear to be as much violent as sexual.

Another curious and sudden threesome, in which Hemmings is one of two men involved this time, is created when he decides to visit his friends across the hall: a painter and his mistress. Unable to discuss his controversial photograph with his editor, who is off on his high, he seeks counsel with this couple and so drops in—to find them busy making love. He is held, before he can back out, by the mistress' glittering eye fixed on him mock-teasingly. In the perspective of *Zabriskie Point*, we can now observe in these scenes with fans and neighbors an adumbration of the latter film's orgy-in-the-desert sequence, whose regiment of lovers is arranged in variously combined groups. And, in their far from sublimely intimate quality, the scenes from *Blow-Up* also anticipate the decided ambiguity of treatment of the desert love-in, which comes across as a vision rather more desperate than celebratory.

In the world of *Blow-Up,* in any case, one aspect of the style of the characters is their easy orientation to ways of sex that are neither private nor personal. As defined by Hemmings and Redgrave in their hurried meeting, the sexual attitudes of all the characters tend to be unromantic and coolly sardonic. In general, the young people act more on reflex than on premeditation. No one lays out structured five-year-plans or plots. As expected, we never see Hemmings preparing to "go out" in any formal way: instead, his world is one in which people randomly drop in and out of scenes.

Except for the presumed slain, gray-haired man in the park and the cranky clerk of an antique shop, none of the people in the film seems to be older than thirty, and most seem to be a good deal younger. A main feeling shared by this world of the young—as it is generally shared by the characters in an Antonioni film—is the desire to be elsewhere: on any turf but the one presently occupied. Thus, everyone is ready for a trip. The young woman who owns the antique shop talks of selling it to afford a flight to ". . . Nepal or Morocco . . ." The hero keeps wishing for enough cash to permit his going in search of a place where he might be "free." In like manner, the young engineer played by Richard Harris in *Red Desert* awaits his trip to Brazil where he, too, hopes to be "free." The heroine of *Red Desert* looks broodingly on the ships in the harbor and the men who sail them. This mass compulsion to flight is the clearest symptom of a time without peace. And, as in times of outright war, relationships remain frankly tentative—pauses along the routes of lone marchers during which messages and news of temporary "Nepals" are relayed. In the antique shop, the object that proves most appropriate to the hero's mood, and that he insists on buying, is a not-very-antique propeller (a found metaphor which will be materialized into the airplane that the hero of *Zabriskie Point* steals for a flight away from Berkeley). Drugs are, of course, in common use since they provide the most readily accessible of "trips."

In the course of his search for the mystery woman of the park, Hemmings is drawn into another game of disassociation from the environment: as one of the crowd at a folk rock concert, he watches while the lead performer smashes his guitar and flings part of it to the howling audience. Hemmings happens to grab hold of this prize, and he uses it to fight his way to the street. In largely reflex action, he thus asserts himself as a winner among the crowd. But this is not freedom. Alone on the street, he hurls away the wooden stump with a violent flourish. Again, we are reminded of the involuntary nature of his earlier involvements and his mixed attitude toward them.

Hemmings' rounds through friends' flats and shops and concert halls lead him full circle back to the park where he had first observed the mystery couple, and from which, overnight, the body discovered in his blow-up had disappeared. All along, he had been drawn in quest of the missing body. But he is at last diverted—decisively—from any such further pursuit by another game, the only one we see him joining without reserve.

The film had opened with shots juxtaposing the hero on his solitary jaunt through the streets of London with the buoyant entry on the streets of a youthful band made up and dressed like clowns. In the final scenes, Hemmings and the revellers are brought together when he stops outside the park's tennis court, occupied by two of the band who, without rackets or balls, mimic a game. While their fellows, in the role of spectators, move their heads from side to side to the tempo of the match, the rhythm itself becomes real on the sound track as we hear the sounds of a tennis ball being struck and bouncing on the court—until it is hit out of court to land, it would seem, right at Hemmings' feet. And now, with his full being as a participant rather than as a coolly detached spectator or as an "operator," Hemmings goes through the motions of scooping up the ball and throwing it back to the players on court, one of whom thanks him before resuming play. Here—in a moment startling in its "peace"—Antonioni finds the ideal shot his hero had failed to get to conclude his book of photographs. Then the camera abruptly arcs high and away from Hemmings in a back-zoom which leaves him looking up from the super-green depths of the park—an anonymous and lilliputian figure in a landscape.[4] The hero's complete disappearance from the field in a final trick shot is perhaps ironically suggestive of the one sort of peace ever possible in an absolute sense: that of a total nonhuman blankness.

III

For some critics, the tennis court finale appears so incongruous in tone to the rest of the film as to be sentimental and arbitrary.[5] Yet the sequence fits squarely into the iconography of Antonioni's films, providing an apt parallel, for example, to the concluding shot of one of the earliest major works, *Il Grido* (*The Outcry*). In this film, a workingman is displaced from the home base of his existence when the woman he had been living with for many years leaves him, without warning, to marry another man. His subsequent wanderings define not so much a real quest on his part as a circling about his lair in a state of shock. He remains, so to say, too heavyset in character to float free of his anchoring sense of reality and "peace." In the last scene, he stares down from a high tower overlooking his empty home, and, with a cry of total despair over his loss, falls to his death.

Hemmings, too, proves to be on a vain, essentially neurotic, quest. He circles about the fatal spot in the park (emptied of the body Hemmings presumed should be there) in the way the workingman circles about his vacant house. For Hemmings, the missing body signifies the loss of a tangible coordinate in reality apart and beyond the games, put-ons, and role-playing involved in his usual rounds. But

[4] This scene was shot on location, but that the real park serves only as a source for the illusion sought—the real world of the location standing in relation to the filmed scene as, say, his sources served Shakespeare for his plays—is emphasized through the much-publicized fact of Antonioni's having had the grass painted over to his specifications. The whole fanciful play in this scene of sound effect and color scheme suggests how much the director himself—like his young protagonist—has here most freely entered into the spirit of the game.

[5] In an interesting essay titled "*Blow-Up*" in *December*, 9 (Chicago, 1967), 142, F. A. Macklin, for example, suggests that this scene ". . . changes the mood and concentration of the film. The clowns seem out of another world . . ." For a contrasting view, on the scene as wholly negative in its connotations, as an image of "disintegration," see Thomas Hernacki, "Antonioni and the Imagery of Disintegration," *Film Heritage*, Spring, 1970, pp. 13–22.

since he is pretty much free-floating to begin with, he can ride with his anxiety in a way the earlier hero cannot. And when he joins in the make-believe tennis game, and so helps bring it into existence as that sort of contemporary art work called a "Happening," he, in one toss, shucks off that obsession with an anchor point which destroys the protagonist of *Il Grido*. Among the various quests which recur throughout the films, we may also note that of the heroine of *L'Avventura,* for her girlfriend mysteriously disappeared from an island. This quest also proves both vain and equivocal in nature, as it becomes clear that what the heroine most seeks is reassurance concerning a friendship she had valued as central to her existence. Indeed, her quest leads to shocks concerning not only her ideals of friendship but also those to do with romantic love—both of which kinds of experience she is brought to seeing in a changed perspective.

From the sort of changed perspectives opened up by a film like *L'Avventura,* we turn with the Happening to an experience that radically qualifies our traditional standards and expectations of art. The Happening neutralizes our sense of the sacrosanct authority of the artist, and our sense of the relationship of the audience to his work, and finally our sense of art in relation to reality. Walls are broken down in the illusion of the game, as what is created through the illusion is another Elsewhere. The real world—which is to say the world from which Everyman presently feels as alienated as the old artist-hero—now becomes merely a starting point, a "source" for Everyman as well as for the artist, as both meet in motive and act in the Happening, "not-always-repugnant-monsters" together! *Blow-Up* thus builds to a scene in which the analogous situation between artist and Everyman, as felt by Antonioni, is made dramatically explicit. The scene falls in place in the context of the whole film as a desperate, fleeting pastoral.

Isolation and Make-Believe
in BLOW-UP
by GEORGE SLOVER

Photography, rock, and pot are so many foci of London's mod world and its "swinging" offshoots in urban centers everywhere. In *Blow-Up*, Antonioni reveals the histrionic basis of the life intent on these foci: its underlying motive is to create a new order out of the sheer willingness to suspend disbelief.

In *Blow-Up* Antonioni also lays bare the terrible pathos which is at once the source and the upshot of this impulse. The concluding parable brings the director's vision into focus. The miming of the clowns creates not just a tennis game but, more fundamentally, a community, a sharing in a super-personal reality. Creation of community is, in fact, the end to which the making-believe is merely the means. The make-believe impulse arises, Antonioni shows, out of the pathos of isolation. When the act of suspending disbelief has run its course, the loner falls back into his estrangement. There is, then, a kind of built-in pathos in the effort to create community by make-believe. It is the lyricism of this anguish which we hear—now faintly, now distinctly—throughout Antonioni's film.

Only once does the photographer-hero (Hemmings, to be designated "H." hereafter) give voice to his underlying malaise. Past the table, in the restaurant where Ron and H. are sitting, a female walks swinging her buttocks provocatively. In detached disgust, H. complains to Ron that he is "off London." If he had money, he says, he would get away

Excerpted from George Slover, "Blow-Up: Medium, Message, Mythos and Make-Believe," The Massachusetts Review 9 *(Autumn 1968): 753–70. Copyright © 1968 by* The Massachusetts Review. *Reprinted by permission of the author. The complete article, from which this excerpt was taken, first appeared in Italian translation in* Strumenti Critici, 5 *(February 1968).*

from it all and be free. What makes this remark so puzzling is that H. *has* money, and if money could buy what H. yearns for, he could probably afford it. The girl who owns the antique shop also wants to get out of London, also feels hemmed in, and appears already headed for Nepal. Perhaps this need to get out of London or out of the antique shop is a cover for another—as yet undefined and hence pathetic— need: to get out of themselves.

To an audience nurtured in the closed-door ethos of the middle class, what is so remarkable in *Blow-Up* is the singular ease with which characters walk into and out of one another's living quarters. All doors appear to be open; locks are out. H. drifts into his painter neighbor's apartment any time of the day or night. There is nothing unusual in his coming upon the painter and his mistress making love. Minutes later, the girl returns the call. So, too, the teeny-boppers, total strangers, appear on the scene uninvited, are put to work making coffee. The person who filches the photos of the murder seems to have no trouble getting in. Studio and apartment, professional models and private friends, working associates, and neighbors, all merge and mingle. The atmosphere suggests the "new tribalism" which Marshall McLuhan is prophesying. The mod world is its vanguard. This new tribalism celebrates openness, receptivity, spontaneity, a sharing of goods, particularly the good of sense experience. At first, the communality Antonioni presents seems convincing and engaging; it is based, apparently, on the various enthusiasms of the mod world: the camera image, music, clothes, pot. There is a rejection of all forms of establishment life, particularly those which divide and repress.

The relationship between H. and V.R. (Vanessa Redgrave) unfolds in this context and in this style. It is an attempt by a lonely young man to make friends—an attempt which never has a chance. From the first, H. is taken with V.R., whether with her freshness and spunk or with the concealed fright which he senses is not important. Like a little boy in his first puppy love, H. offers V.R. his most precious possession: he proposes to make a model of her, tells her she's a natural, has her stand against the lavender paper, then sit on the sofa, as if he were administering a screen test. He puts on a record, offers her a cigarette, presumably marijuana; teaches her how to get the most out of it by inhaling "against the beat" of the music. These are acts of friendship; he is taking her under his wing. Anxious to retrieve the film, however, V.R. sends H. for a drink of water, grabs the camera and runs. H. intercepts her at the bottom of the stairs. Still misunderstanding H.'s motives, she takes off her blouse and offers herself as swap for the film. Seeing that she will settle for nothing less—and still unwilling to part with the park shots, and perhaps also persuaded that there is nothing compromising of V.R. on the film, whatever she may think—H. goes to the dark room and returns with a bogus roll of film. Thinking she has what she came for, V.R. relaxes. She permits her affinity for the photographer to surface. She invites H. to make love—not because she has to, but because she wants to. In the last scene of the sequence, she is again sitting on the sofa across from her coach, smoking and laughing spontaneously. Suddenly she looks at her watch, jumps up, gets dressed. H. asks for her name and phone number. She scribbles something on a piece of paper, gives it to him and goes.

The scene is marvelously constructed to reveal the rhythm between friendship and estrangement, between community and isolation [Plate VIII]. In H. and V.R., Antonioni presents two desperately isolated people reaching for one another. The mod style—music, pot, and cool sex (a style both understand)—serves as ground of their community. Their association is, however, a make-believe. The suspension of disbelief cannot dissipate the commitments that separate them. Both lovers lay claim to the photos H. shot in the park. And these claims are absolutely irreconcilable. H. claims the photos in the name of art, and thus feels justified in passing off a phony roll of film. H.'s deception makes explicit the gulf that separates them, even though it does not come to be felt until later—until, presumably, V.R. discovers she has been deceived. To V.R., the photos are, simply, evidence of the murder in which she is herself, whatever the details, an accomplice. She claims the photos in the name of life and liberty—her own. Like the film H. gives her, the name and phone number she gives H. turn out later to be fake. The unbridgeable abyss opens. In the last episode of the relationship, H. comes upon V.R. by chance; she is window-shopping. As he goes in pursuit of her, V.R. disappears. The sudden flowering of community in H.'s studio withers again into isolation.

The rhythm which Antonioni presents in H.'s relation to V.R., reverberates through many of *Blow-Up*'s shorter episodes. The painter's mistress, who had earlier given H. a beer and a neck rub, cannot bring herself to tell H. her troubles; she, too, fails to break out of her isolation—sensing, as I have suggested, H.'s preoccupation at that point with his lost photos. The same terrible feeling of sudden estrangement pervades the episode in which the teeny-boppers are shown putting on their hero's socks and making their exit. The mood is in sharp contrast to the comradely sex frolic—community sex, share and share alike— which has preceded. The open doors, the new tribalism of the studio-community, do not, it appears, open souls.

Perhaps the most compelling of the community-isolation images is the pot party sequence. We see, at first, clusters of people seemingly in high communion. Gathered around a little mound of marijuana, they are partaking of the "sacrament": one puffs on a cigarette, another rolls one. H.'s conversation with his collaborator Ron belies this impression. Having found Ron at last, H. tries to communicate the distressing ambiguity he has felt since his awful discovery. A creature of the image, H. is not used to expressing himself in words; he needs to be "drawn out." He has sensed that of all the people he knows Ron could do this. But Ron is "turned on." He misses H.'s point, takes H.'s words— we've got to get a shot of it—at face value; is deaf to the cry for help in them. Hence, the pathetically irrelevant though perfectly logical answer: "Well, I'm not the photographer." With this, Ron walks away, and to make the point secure, Antonioni has Ron mutter to himself, "What did he say?" H. recognizes in Ron's behavior the time and memory distortion of marijuana, gives up the effort to communicate, and accepts Ron's invitation to "turn on" himself. Apparently, the "communion" of the pot party is more a collocation of discrete bodies —a Brownian movement, forming and reforming human clusters at random. It is a make-believe communion. There is as much reality in it as there is in the model's faith that she is in Paris: real absence, it might be called, or perfect isolation.

There is in the mod mode of life a hellish futility. The make-believe impulse aimed at creating community deepens, when enacted, the very isolation with which the impulse is to cope. In *Blow-Up* Antonioni penetrates to the source of the compulsion which powers this infernal mechanism.

Once again, the clowns furnish the pattern in little. The mimes stand in high relief against the world in which they move. They constitute a community within, yet over-against, the larger community. They depend, however, on that community; depend on it precisely as performers depend on their audience. In the film's first sequence, they take up a collection for their performance, as if the miming were their livelihood. In the clowns' relation to their audience is figured the relationship between the mod community and the establishment.

Curiously, the action of *Blow-Up* unfolds almost entirely within the mod community; the establishment is hardly represented directly. Characters over thirty are very few: the down-and-outs in the doss house, off-scourings of the establishment—who are used to indict it; the elderly salesman in the antique shop who turns out to be not the owner but an employee of the young woman who owns and is selling the shop; finally, the murdered man, about whom, more in a moment. Though not directly represented, the larger community is, nevertheless, everywhere implied in *Blow-Up*; indeed, the mod community is everywhere dependent on it. To begin with, mod depends on the establishment for technology. Consider the highly sophisticated and marvelous photographic equipment in H.'s studio and laboratory. Not just mod's image culture, but also its music culture is technologized. And Antonioni makes a point of showing us the fact: the large amplifier with its knobs and dials which the electric-guitar player pummels again and again in his rage over its imperfect operation. Consider also the crucial role of the automobile in the mod world as represented in *Blow-Up*. Mobility, the mastery of space, is of the essence. Antonioni gives the hero's Rolls Royce considerable attention, shows it in action again and again, even equips it with a two-way radio. In the same vein, Antonioni mobilizes his company of clowns with a kind of jeep—the first machine we see in the film. The mod world and the mod culture presuppose the square technology of the square establishment. The establishment is a hovering presence, as is the invisible audience in a theater to actors on a stage.

Like the clowns, the mod community Antonioni presents does, in fact, earn its keep from the surrounding society. Antonioni's hero, we may have already remarked, is a man of some means: his car, his living arrangements, his working conditions, all bear witness. Indeed, there is no real poverty in the mod community. H. is both an artist and commercial. His collaboration with Ron on the photographic essay—which is "art"—may or may not net some income. But surely the fashion photos and the sex shots are big money-makers, and it is the establishment that pays. The mod community functions, first of all, as costumers to the establishment. The outfits Antonioni selects reveal to what taste mod designers are appealing: the taste for fantasy. The fashions H. photographs belong to a science fiction world, cut off from ordinary experience. As a fashion photographer, H. is an indispensable middleman. His job is to catalyze the imagination of the larger community and to induce women to enter into mod's fantasy world. We know, in fact, how marketable these clothes are. The sex photos, also marketable, have a function similar to the fashion shots. In the mod community sex has already "cooled off"; in the establishment it is still "hot"—a discrepancy which the mod community is quick to exploit for commercial purposes. H. and his like keep the establishment imagination (inhibited by discipline) supplied with images of delight, abandon, passion, freedom; no matter that they are fantasy images.

Mod is, in fact, a kept community—kept by the establishment, and kept, precisely, for its special skill in making believe. Completely com-

mitted to a life of calculations—scientific, technical, industrial, economic—the establishment generates an unappeasable appetite for fantasy. Paradoxically, the sober creators of technology require, for sheer
human survival, the intoxicated creators of fantasy. Thus the depend-
ency is mutual. One might see in this phenomenon the application of
the division of labor to man's *inner* economy. Establishment life causes
atrophying, in its members, of certain functions of the soul—the life of
the senses, of the imagination, of the feelings. Instinctively, the establishment generates and fosters a community, necessarily separate,
which will cultivate these powers. The result is the coexistence of two
communities with two mutually exclusive, yet mutually dependent,
ideals of man.[1] But more, the establishment fosters the creation of a
make-believe world in which those powers of the soul can live their life
insulated from those other, calculating and narrowly rational, powers
which the establishment cultivates as appropriate to *its* fantasy of the
world.

Viewed structurally, mod is nothing new: it is merely the latest in a
long succession of Bohemias which make good. As a Bohemia, it is a
community in which the "artist" is king and priest and in which the
rest of the members subserve the creative process in one way or another,
if only as an audience which guarantees approval. What makes *Blow-Up*
such an extraordinary work of art is that it gets to the bottom of the
Bohemian psychology and mythology. Like the clowns of the film, the
mod community is organized as a theatrical troupe; the establishment,
the society at large, is at once its audience and its employer (and as employer, it pays better than the patrons of former Bohemias). On the
surface, the arrangement seems plausible enough. Antonioni reveals,
however (and he is himself a member of Bohemia), that, appearance
notwithstanding, this arrangement is deadly, certainly for the artist but
probably also for his audience—fraught with contradiction and conflict.

The Bohemian community—mod or otherwise—arises out of the
artist's pathos of isolation, his alienation from, and rejection by the
larger community. The act of make-believe through which the anti-
community comes into being is attended by large measures of anger,
reverse rejection, revolt. *Épater le bourgeois* is the order of the day.
The artist is pure; the bourgeois, corrupt (the very spirit we discern in
H.'s doss house pictures). Indeed, after a decade or more of angry and
absurd theatre, we are familiar with playwrights' and actors' ways of
abusing the audience that patronizes them. Give that audience time,

---

[1] This phenomenon of the industrial age has recently received considerable attention in the discussion evoked by C. P. Snow's *The Two Cultures and the Scientific Revolution* (New York: Cambridge University Press, 1956).

however, and it will come to love it. That is what is paradoxical—may I say, pathological?—in this state of affairs. What has happened to a whole chain of Bohemias and what is happening to mod is that the establishment—confused by the outburst of hostility, uncomprehending, feeling victimized—responds in the only way it knows how: by putting Bohemia on the payroll. This parody of turning the other cheek has, *Blow-Up* suggests, a certain psychological impact on the members of the "artistic" community: a progressive deepening of alienation, a confirming of "coolness" (passive aggressive, in the lingo of interpersonal psychology), leading to a total rupture of communications between the communities. In individuals, this rupture takes the form, first, of ontologizing the act of make-believe—the act Antonioni performs for us in having H. *hear* the report of the imaginary tennis ball; second, of de-ontologizing the world which furnishes the artist his material—H.'s annihilation of the body.

One is tempted to place *Blow-Up*'s murder into this context. What is so provocative about the murder is Antonioni's selection of personnel. In his short story, Julio Cortázar stages the park drama between an older, mature woman and an adolescent of perhaps seventeen. The third party is an older man sitting in a near-by car for whose perverse sexual interest the older woman is presumably soliciting the young man. Antonioni changes all this around. He gives us an older, already greying, man lured by a very young woman to a spot where he is shot by a third party. If this third person is the young man whom H. catches peeping in on him and Ron through the restaurant window, then the murderer, too, is under twenty-five. The older man—one of the very few characters over thirty, as we have already said—is also clearly establishment. He wears a well-tailored suit with vest, white shirt, tie. The girl, on the other hand, is clearly mod: mini-skirt worn from the hip. In the unfolding of the film, the viewer begins by surmising that a solid businessman type has fallen for a young mod, or that a precocious young mod is deliberately turning the head of an older man for fun or fortune. Antonioni misleads us intentionally: we witness, in fact, a premeditated murder plot in which the woman is decoy for bringing the victim into range of a revolver. What appears as a charming flirtation between the communities—over thirty and under twenty-five, establishment and mod—is, in fact, the murder of the old by the young, the destruction of the keeper by the kept. The murder is the physical analogue of H.'s spiritual annihilation of the corpse in the final sequence.

In both scenes, Antonioni enacts (if we read him aright) the final rupture between the communities, the irrevocable estrangement. We have already noted that Antonioni places the murder in an idyll, in a garden. This, too, represents a change from the Cortázar story where the photographed scene takes place by a parapet overlooking the river within view of a parked automobile. Is Antonioni alluding to the garden story in *Genesis* where likewise is enacted the drama of an irrevocable estrangement? If so, we can discern in *Blow-Up* the comprehensive mythos of mod Bohemia: a mythos which unfolds in two great symbolic acts. The first is the primordial act which effects the estrangement of the two communities. The second is the act through which the hero "saves" himself from the painful consequences of the primordial estrangement. In the first, a man is murdered; in the second, the existence of the man is denied by making believe that his corpse is real only to art, on film. The latter act is, however, the parody of a saving act: it confirms the initial act by de-ontologizing its consequence. In *Blow-Up*, Antonioni performs for us the two cultic acts—sacrifice and initiation —of the religion which makes art the comprehensive mystery; the artist its high priest; Bohemia its church; the establishment its world. The estrangement of the two communities may be taken as the ultimate source of the pathetic, lingering isolation which afflict so many characters in *Blow-Up*'s mod world. That pervasive alienation is to the murder and make-believe in *Blow-Up* as sin and disorder is to the disobedience of the garden in the Judaeo-Christian scheme. Estrangement within the primordial community is prior, ontologically, to estrangement of individuals from one another and within themselves.

Perhaps this is pushing things too far. Nevertheless, this much remains secure: *Blow-Up* presents the estrangement both of mod from the establishment and of the members of the mod community from one another. In the theatricalizing impulse, Antonioni reveals the source of this estrangement. The chief "objective correlative" of the film's master motive is the camera and the "photographic mode of life." The camera, make-believe, and the pathetic sense of estrangement—these three, *Blow-Up* brings into significant relationship.

And yet, there is *no necessary connection* between alienation and making believe. The fact is that the theatricalizing impulse is enormously rich. We discern its working in numberless instances within our daily experience. Long before *Blow-Up*, poets, playwrights, novelists explored its appeal and its meaning. Long ago, the notions "life is a play" and "the world is a theatre" were commonplaces. One already encounters them in Plato and Democritus, and finds them cropping up again and again since that time down to the Renaissance and beyond. Nevertheless, these ages understood the life-acting and the world-theatre equations as metaphor, and theatricality as one of many modes of human activity. What Antonioni presents in *Blow-Up* is a community which construes the whole of human life as theatrical. For mod, the theatre-world equation is no longer metaphor; it is literally so. Its make-believe, when acted, generates *in fact* a social order radically divided and estranged, generates *in fact* an isolation terrible in its completeness. *Blow-Up* gives the theatrical impulse a very special turn. . . .

BLOW-UP:
From the Word to the Image
by JOHN FRECCERO

In the vocabulary of the communication arts, the word "linear" has come to have a pejorative meaning, standing for a mode of expression, indeed for an entire culture which seems to have been superseded. Linearity and sequence have given way to graphic totality, the written word to audio-visual communication and literature itself, long since displaced as the medium of popular escapism, sees its survival threatened even among the intellectual elite. The current popularizers of the cultural revolution are of course the McLuhanites, but the attack of film estheticians took place much earlier and was both more subtle and more sustained. The burden of their critique was that literature, far from enriching the new visual medium, was in fact a contamination.

Recently, the argument seems to have become more embittered by having been ignored for so long by the academy. Andrew Sarris, for instance, writing in the *New York Times,* noted petulantly that the literary establishment has at long last discovered the film, is trying desperately to claim it as its own, but that such efforts are futile: "No serious scholar of the film is too concerned with the sudden conversion of the *littérateurs.*" The implication seems to be that the superannuated students of literature had best stick to their obsolete discipline and make way for the cultural revolution.

In part, of course, the anti-literary polemic has been sustained by the vagueness of its terms. Sometimes the word "literary" seems to refer to narrative clichés or to the official culture traditionally charged with embalming them. At other times, words themselves seem to be under attack and "literature" is taken to mean the verbal medium in general.

From Yale/Theatre *3 (Fall 1970): 15–24. Copyright* © *1970 by* Yale/
Theatre. *Reprinted by permission of the author.*

For all the confusion, however, the tone is much too shrill not to betray a certain anxiety among film estheticians about the nature of their own medium. It is traditional to point out that the film is distinct from, say, both the novel and the theater in that it is a visual, often representational medium (unlike written literature), but with a technically mediated, constantly shifting and completely controlled perspective. At the same time, it is equally obvious that the film is a system of communication that functions, even when it is totally silent, very much like language itself. As early as Sergei Eisenstein and a generation or so before the advent of semiotics, it was recognized that selection and combination, the twin characteristics of the linguistic act, were analogous to Eisenstein's description of the process of montage, or editing, while the double articulation of language is already implicit in his distinction between photographic *representation,* comparable to the phoneme, and the *image,* the result of an interpretation and therefore comparable to a unit of meaning. When Eisenstein illustrated his principles of montage with a translation of some verses of Pushkin into a hypothetical silent "shooting script," he effectively demonstrated certain undeniable affinities between literature, understood both poetically and linguistically, and the new art form which he helped to create.

My purpose in outlining some of these elements of the debate about literature and film is not to enter that debate directly, but rather to introduce my subject, Michelangelo Antonioni, whose work seems to be surrounded by precisely the same controversy. While Antonioni has been popularly upbraided for his incomprehensibility and dullness, what one wag has referred to as "antoniennui," several film experts have accused him of what seems to be an opposite fault: that is, of being too literary and too pat.

One Italian critic goes so far as to denounce his "literary corruption," thus adding the moral indignation of the film theorist to that of the censors and assuring a *succès de scandale* in the sophisticated periodicals as well as at the box-office. So an evaluation of an Antonioni film inevitably rehashes the traditional polemic and revives the old confusions, with partisans defending the stark visual virtuosity and detractors pointing to the literary sentimentality of the creative genius whose work seems as problematic as the principles of the medium in which he works.

The quality of Antonioni's films was a subject of heated debate long before the appearance of *Blow-Up,* the film which both intensified the debate and shifted it to a more popular forum. All the critics agreed that the film marked a radical departure from Antonioni's previous idiom, both visually and thematically. For one thing, Monica Vitti was missing. For another, swinging London seemed to lend more visual movement to this film than to any of his others. Finally, perhaps most startling, this film seemed to have a plot, or almost, and the first half of it prompted some to speak of it as though it were alienated Hitchcock. Put most simply, while nothing ever seemed to happen in *L'Avventura*, *La Notte, L'Eclisse*, or *II Deserto Rosso*, here at last something had indeed happened, although it was difficult to say with any assurance what it was. For the film theorist, the radical change in subject matter marked a thematic change of great importance. Because the leading character is a photographer who attempts to interpret his own work, it appeared that the director had left off his exploration of neurosis and alienation in order to make his own entry, however oblique, into the debate about the nature of his own medium.

Blow-Up is in fact a series of photographs about a series of photographs and so constitutes what might be called a metalinguistic metaphor, a highly self-conscious and self-reflexive meditation on its own process. Because it is a discourse about discourse, it is subject to all the charges of ambiguity that are usually levelled at such self-contained messages, even when they occur in everyday speech. At the same time, however, that ambiguity places it within a literary tradition, founded perhaps by Petrarch, in which literature's subject is itself and the portrait of the artist is his act.

There can be no doubt that Antonioni's mod photographer, Thomas, is in fact an artist—primarily a visual artist. Early in the film, a scene at the house of his painter friend establishes a symbolic equation between their respective techniques. Bill is contemplating one of the paintings that differs markedly from all his other work in that it contains a figurative element, or what seems to be one:

> While I'm doing them, they don't say anything to me—just one big mess. After a while I find something to hang onto. Like that leg there. Then it comes through by itself. It's like finding the key in a mystery story.

For those who fail to recall those lines when the photographer examines his own work, Antonioni has Patricia, the painter's companion, restate the equation when she sees the photographic blow-up: "It looks just like one of Bill's paintings." When he is first introduced, Bill would seem to be the photographer's antitype, a loser trying desperately to keep his painting, which Thomas jocularly threatens to steal, and his woman, who wants desperately to be stolen. By the film's ending, it becomes evident that the parallel is exact, for Thomas too has lost both his work of art, which is stolen, and the woman he coveted who is somehow responsible for its loss.

As a visual artist, however, Thomas differs markedly from the painter and even from his fellow photographers in that he aspires to totality. He seeks to transcend time and to achieve the self-containment and the autonomy of a world created by his camera rather than illustrated by it. This, I take it, is the sense of a detail which most critics of the film have overlooked but which seems to me essential. One of the first things we learn about Thomas and the reason why he finds himself in the park, at the scene of the crime where he makes his discovery, is that he is putting together, structuring, a *book* of photographs. Thomas differs from his photographer colleagues, whose craft is documentary, in that his gaze transforms the representation of reality into its image, an interpretive act resembling that of the painter. He differs from the painter, however, in that he introduces the temporality of syntax into his art, juxtaposing images into a structure along a syntagmatic axis, which is the essence of language or, for that matter, of montage. Had he succeeded in putting together his book of images and achieving a real simulacrum of time, he would have come very close to resembling the film maker who has been accused of excessively literary preoccupation.

However veiled the allegory and however arch the transposition, the confessional suggestiveness of the story is the unmistakable consequence of the metalinguistic metaphor. As long as one remains within a narrative structure, then the story that tells its own story is perfectly self-contained. When stories are great art, however, and not myth, they come into existence through a consciousness that exists as story-teller: to tell the story of how the story came into existence is necessarily to portray the story-teller, no matter how metaphorically, just as the story-teller's autobiography, as story-teller, is the story he tells. So with Antonioni's meditation on his own art: Thomas is perhaps the portrait of the director as a young director and his failure is Antonioni's subsequent triumph.

The structure is familiar in literature, from Dante to Proust, and was recently introduced into the film by Federico Fellini, the title of whose cinematic autobiography, *8½*, points unmistakably to the fact that it is a retrospective attempt to understand his own work. The story is of a director who, while fearing that he is washed up after what seems to him to have been a fragmentary career, nevertheless is filming a film that is in fact the film we view. Most interesting from our standpoint, however, is the conclusion of *8½*, where the director is called upon to sum it all up, both as character and as director, and to give significance to all that went before. Finding himself unable finally to do this, he crawls under the banquet table where he is being honored and shoots himself, whereupon he is immediately resurrected in time to conduct his band of mimes and *pagliacci* in the parade that is Fellini's trademark, the *Trionfo*, so to speak, of illusion over reality.

Fellini the *magus* hides his human despair, just as do his characters, behind the mask of the lie; in this case, the phony suicide, which both gives a conclusiveness to his life story and grants him, author and *persona*, the leisure and the Archimedean point outside of time from which to tell it. It is this compromise with authenticity, the willing embrace of the lie inherent in the medium itself, that Antonioni has always refused. Fellini perhaps set up the problematic, the cinematic code, and Antonioni perhaps assumes it, for film makers, no less than writers, must work within a tradition; nevertheless, the bittersweet of Fellini's lie is rejected and the code is assumed only to be destroyed. In his preface to a collection of six screen plays, Antonioni had written: "The greatest danger for the film maker consists in the extraordinary means the medium provides in order to lie." *Blow-Up* is the dramatic refutation of Fellini's make-believe and its bleakness consists in the fact that the only alternatives it offers to the lie are the search or silence.

To make the point about the metaphoric relationship between the director and his protagonist a little more convincingly, I should like for a moment to go outside the "text." In an interview on Italian television, Antonioni was asked why, when he knew it would cost him ecclesiastical approval in Italy, he included in the film the photographer's orgy with a pair of teeny-boppers. He replied that while he was not at all averse to incurring the displeasure of the censors, he really had something else in mind. In a world as notoriously alienated and neurotic as his own, he felt the need to provide some relief with an episode of good clean fun. The television interviewer was an ideal straight-man, since he had not seen the film and therefore could not catch the irony. Even the most casual viewing of the film would have revealed that it is precisely for the same reason, to find some erotic relief from a gloomy world, that Thomas goes into the park in the first place. His book of photographs includes a series of portraits of derelict old men in a public dormitory, most of them more or less close to death. In order to relieve the grimness of his photographs, which he senses with some detachment, he goes into an Arcadian scene, a park with an enclosed garden, where he photographs a pair of lovers. It is only later that he discovers, with the retrospective gaze of the artist interpreting his own work, that he has in fact portrayed not the embrace of lovers, but the death of an older man. In short, the fact of death which he had been seeking to evade. Had he seen Poussin or read Panofsky, he would have known that this disillusionment awaits all attempts at pastoral evasion: "Et in Arcadia ego." Death resides even in Arcady [Plate X].

What makes the photographer symbolically capable of making that discovery is of course a discovery about himself. The interpretative act of the artist does not depend so much on the physical evidence as on the construct which one is ready to bring to it and before Thomas can understand, his own authenticity must be questioned. This occurs in his orgy with the aspiring models, who stand chronologically in relationship to him as does the girl, Vanessa Redgrave, to the older man for whose death she is somehow responsible. By a cinematic tour de force, Antonioni presents us with the visual equivalent of one of the oldest *double-entendre* of erotic poetry: to die, the orgasm as the moment of death. Lying prostrate on the floor of his studio after his debauch, the photographer looks up and discovers, or thinks that he discovers, the erstwhile older lover lying in the photograph in precisely the same position. He does not as yet suspect what the audience has already grasped: just as Thomas is the metaphoric embodiment of Antonioni's art, so the older man is the metaphoric embodiment of Thomas' art. The dead man is the dead-end conclusion of Thomas' book and thus, symbolically, an all too definitive portrait of the artist which cannot be revived by cinematographic sleight-of-hand.

The photograph of lovers in the park was to be not only pastoral relief in Thomas' book, but its very conclusion. When they meet in a restaurant to discuss the photographs, Ron, the photographer's friend and publisher, asks him which of the photographs of the older men he would like to put last. Thomas, who does not as yet suspect what his films contain, replies:

> None of these. I have something fabulous to wind up with. In a park. I took them this morning. Let you have them tonight. There's a silence in them, a peace . . . The rest of the book is violent enough and maybe it would be better to end it this way . . .

It is this sense of the ending, of poetic closure, that marks Thomas as a literary man, an expert in montage, like a formalist literary critic who wishes to achieve a balance and a symmetry in his interpretation. The subsequent discovery, that of the death in the park, takes him far beyond formalism, however. If the aspiration of the artist is to express himself in a formal structure, with an ending that is both neat and authentic, what in his life can possibly correspond to finality in montage, unless it is death?

The silence that ends his adventure in the park is like the syntactic silence of Merleau-Ponty or, before him, of St. Augustine, who first established the parallel between the unfolding of the sentence and the progress of the soul. For Augustine, the eternity of the Platonists was the world of pure form, too abstracted and remote to be of existential concern to men. The time of the flesh, on the other hand, was the chaos of unintelligibility, a tale told by an idiot, signifying nothing. Between these extremes there stands the word, as the Word of God stands between eternity and time, syntax as time redeemed and pressed into the service of significance. As the phoneme derives meaning retrospectively with unfolding sound, so too do the words and the entire sentence and the discourse as a whole, whose significance falls into place only at its conclusion. Insofar as language is not extrinsic to man but part of his very nature, so the linearity of syntax is an emblem of human time and death gives meaning retrospectively to life. Under such circumstances, it is difficult to see how anyone would even attempt autobiography. Life can of course be the metaphor for the book, just as the book can be the metaphor for life; even writers seem to be interested in both. The point is that the dual finality in a single literary structure is inconceivable. It is perhaps for this reason that Jean Paul Sartre's autobiography, *Les Mots* is deliberately open-ended. Short of an Augustinian spiritual death and resurrection, the syntactic silence that follows life precludes sharing the significance with others.

The same is perhaps true of the cinematic genre founded by Fellini. Insofar as it pretends to capture autobiography within a complete structure—and films must be complete—it is doomed to failure for the same reason that makes it impossible to take inventory before the store is closed to business. If we object that this does not apply to spiritual autobiography by the novelist or film maker, whose metaphoric biography is simply his definitive statement about his own art, then the problem is attenuated, but no less absurd: the artist can make no definitive statement about his art until he ceases to be an artist, which excludes his definitive statement from its own corpus. It is in this sense that the logical absurdity of the definitive book matches the logical absurdity of definitive autobiography. There seem to be only two ways out of this dilemma: either to deny any point of tangency between illusion and reality and embrace the lie with full creative awareness, as does Fellini, or to dramatize the dilemma with a surrogate in search of a conclusion, a film about its own impossibility, like the dead body which Thomas no sooner touches than it disappears. Antonioni, like Marx, insists that truth resides not simply in the goal, but in the process whereby one approaches it, even if it is never attained. He writes: "A director does nothing more than search for himself in his films. The films are not the record of a completed thought, but rather that very thought in the making."

This is the Antonionian search which finds visual incarnation in so many of his films, where nothing happens and perhaps nothing ever will happen. What happens in *Blow-Up*, however, happens to an artist who, by the film's ending, has ceased to exist except as Antonioni's counterstatement. The technical process of the blow-up is obviously the metaphor of the search, no longer dramatized in exterior terms as a neurotic odyssey, but as an experience that the Middle Ages would have called the journey *intra nos*. Antonioni had long been fascinated by the metaphor. Three years before the appearance of the film he had used it as an example of the search for the truth in the image. After describing the process in technical detail, he glosses its significance: "We know that beneath the revealed image there is another, more faithful to reality, and beneath this still another, and once more another. Up to the true image of reality itself, absolute, mysterious, which no one will ever see. Or perhaps up to the decomposition of any image at all, of any reality at all. In this sense, even abstract cinema would find its raison d'être." This perhaps makes it clear that Antonioni intended his photographer to achieve his most creative moment not behind his lens, but at the enlarger. After Thomas' suspicions about the lovers' tryst are aroused, he begins to examine details of the prints arranged in sequence around his walls, first with a magnifying glass and then by successively blowing up one of the details to the point where it seems to be nothing but a series of black and white blotches. At that moment he sees, or he thinks he sees, the man being manoeuvred into position for an assassin's bullet from behind a hedge. The interpretation would have been impossible without the interpretive context, which casts the photographer in his self-conceived heroic role and prepares the audience for a mystery story conclusion. Thereafter, both are disappointed, the photographer to discover he did not actually prevent a crime and the audience to discover that it is the body, the reality, which is the object of the search and not whodunit.

Antonioni's rejection of Fellini's joyful prestidigitation is on both metaphysical and sociological grounds, an indictment not only of a cinematic technique but of the whole world of graphic inauthenticity. Thomas lives in a world of which he is king and, virtually, creator. Models are puppets in his hand which, like Hoffman's dolls, come to life only at his command. He tells them to shut their eyes and so they remain while he seeks some distraction. The image is power in swinging London and he is the image maker, mistaking the synchronic, graphic cut through reality that is his own creation for his very life.

The public consequence of this private presumption is his role, not as king of the image, but as peddler. The sub-plot involving the antique shop, which the photographer wants to buy, portrays him as something of a pusher of evasion. The bric-a-brac of another time is a store house of used images waiting to be rearranged by the skillful *bricolage* of the photographer into marketable images, camp, for the new campy inhabitants of the decaying neighborhood. The old man who runs the store, a custodian of the past, refuses to sell him anything [Plate V], but the young girl, who is presumably inheriting it, as the young always do, will sell him anything, just to get away:

> I want to try something else. Go away. I'm sick of antiques.
> Go where?
> To Nepal.
> Nepal is full of antiques!
> Then maybe Morocco would be better.

When the photographer finally buys something from her, it is an old airplane propeller, a symbol of flight, but he wishes to hang it in his studio as a fitting emblem of the place where magic-carpets are put together in the twentieth century.

The photographer's arrogance reaches its height, however, when he concludes in his dark room that his presence in the park actually prevented the crime from taking place. After the visit of Vanessa Redgrave, he discovers the killer and calls his friend Ron to announce: "Listen, I saved a man's life!" Before Thomas can describe in detail what happened, however, he is interrupted by the arrival of the two teenagers who, in spite of their youth, or perhaps because of it, are the occasion for the photographer's discovery of the dead body.

According to our mythology, it was after the fall in the garden of Eden, that sexuality first entered the world and with it entered death. According to the Church Fathers, the act whereby a man asserted his manhood was the same act whereby he entered the cycle of generation and corruption that indicated, unmistakably, how transient his life would be, how soon he would have to make way on the generational line for his own children and those of others. For various reasons, we no longer perceive the connection between sexuality and death with the same immediacy that critics tell us our literary ancestors felt; and we are unaware, perhaps, in indirect proportion to our age. Thomas is twenty-five, so that his absolutely indiscriminate sexuality is what one might expect both of a young man who thinks he will live forever and of an artist who has as yet felt no limitation on what he takes to be the transcendence of his art. The fact that the film is absorbed with his coming of age, however, indicates that his creator is middle-aged. The photographer's *prise de conscience*, both as artist and man, comes about by a kind of triangulation or bracketing, where coordinates are determined visually by splitting the difference between a point that clearly falls short and a point that clearly exceeds the target. He emerges from the category of youth when, after making love to teen-agers, he remarks to Vanessa Redgrave: "Your boy-friend is a little past it, isn't he?" His intention is obviously to suggest that, in point of age, he would be an ideal companion for her. For the first time in the film, Thomas assumes an identity that is not just his artistic tran-scendence, but rather that locates him exactly on a time line with all other mortals and this one in particular. When he first saw her in the garden he was fascinated. There, as in so many literary gardens of the Middle Ages and the Renaissance, Narcissus discovers an image of him-self and thinks he has fallen in love.

Vanessa Redgrave is the first woman whom the photographer seems genuinely to desire and whom he treats, almost, as another human be-ing. Until her appearance in the film, Thomas' sexuality seems as dehumanized as his art, the sexuality of the voyeur (a metaphor for novelistic detachment at least as old as Chaucer), who so transcends his own mortality that he can achieve satisfaction merely by observing, like some God, from a privileged perspective. So he makes love to the model Verushka with his camera or, alternately, frolics with the little girls wrapped in the purple paper he uses for his back-drop. So too, he looks at the pleading eyes of Patricia while she somewhat distractedly allows Bill to make love to her. This last scene is virtually a literary topos: in Chaucer's *Troilus and Creseyde*, when the loving couple are finally in bed together, Pandarus keeps them company while he retires to the fireside to read his old romance. Here, while Patricia and Bill are making love, Thomas turns to look once more at Bill's nearly figura-tive painting to see what it reveals. The technology may differ some-what, but the mechanism is the same.

With Vanessa Redgrave, on the other hand, he finds a kindred spirit whose identity and past are as mysterious as his own. Antonioni under-scores their complementarity even by their dress, for in the scene that provided the publicity stills, the whiteness of her bare flesh and her blue skirt are the colors, symmetrically reversed, in which he is dressed —blue shirt and white slacks—while both she and Thomas are wear-ing identical belts. As they stand in the doorway of the bedroom, the scene seems to be set for what might have been the only completely human encounter of the film, but they are interrupted in a moment that, in another cinematic atmosphere, might have provided comic re-lief—the delivery of the propeller which Thomas had purchased at the antique store. The almost funny moment marks the intrusion of Thomas' vocation and the evasion of reality that it represents. By the parallelism that the film has established between the artist's sexuality and his art, the failure of human love, or at least human contact is exactly equivalent to the failure of his work to achieve humanity.

The meeting with Vanessa Redgrave proves to be an amorous disillusion, so that once she disappears from the studio, she no longer has any part to play in the film. After Thomas' discovery that the story was not quite as he had envisioned it, the audience discovers that the plot of the film is not the suspense story *it* had been led to expect. The object of Thomas' search is not the killers or the perpetrators of the plot, but the body itself, the authenticity of which he had caught a glimpse in the park. The search is a familiar one in the artistic work of which Thomas is the metaphor, the search of the heroine in *L'Avventura,* the spiritual odyssey of *Il Grido,* but in this film, the truth of Antonioni's revelation is briefly revealed in the moment when the photographer touches the body, as if to feel the point of tangency between reality and his art. Antonioni's sociological indictment finds expression again in the photographer's frantic search for some solidarity in order to sustain him in his investigation. As the revelation had been achieved by a kind of bracketing, so he turns to society in the same order, first to the young, who are drugged joylessly by their music, and then to the older, drugged by their cocktails and marijuana. In each of these episodes, the photographer is momentarily taken in by the collective, conditioned desires of the society around him and each time, rediscovering himself as alone in his knowledge, he moves away from his surroundings in despair and disgust. The guitar, smashed by the musician, becomes valorized by the frenzy of his young fans and the photographer joins in the struggle to possess it. Once free of the mob, he throws the worthless bits away. Like the airplane propeller, the intrinsic worth of the object is nil, but it is given value by the collective desire imposed on the crowd by image peddlers. This analysis of London night life, which dismayed English audiences, is the image of a world possessed by a kind of madness that seems to blind it to the fundamental fact of death, in art as in life. The demons of this evasion inhabit the entire world of mass media, they are its spirits, and so they begin and end Antonioni's film.

The film opens at dawn with a group of students, extravagantly dressed, presumably for Rag Week, their faces painted white, who descend from their jeep and scatter to inhabit the whole of the city. Like the *Untorelli* of Manzoni's *Promessi Sposi,* their mission seems to be to spread the plague whose name is perhaps best established by the strange protest sign GO AWAY, that one of them gives to the photographer as he speeds away from the desolation of the public dormitory. The same students close the film in the famous and problematic ending, again at dawn, where some watch and others play a phantom tennis match without a ball. Thomas watches the students, at first with amusement, as they follow with dead seriousness and the same joyless and empty look that he had previously seen at the rock session, the flight of an imaginary ball. When the phantom ball seems to have gone outside the court, presumably at his feet, they plead with him with their eyes to return it. He hesitates, finally stoops as if to pick something up, weighs it in his hand and finally throws it back, thus collaborating in their phantom game. As he walks slowly away, the sound of a tennis ball against a racket can clearly be heard, and the camera moves slowly away from the minute figure of the photographer until he quite literally disappears before our eyes.

The demonic character of the students can scarcely be doubted. Their fantastic dress, their appearance at dawn, their white faces, their station in life and weird behavior mark them clearly as what anthropologists would call "marginal" figures, the demons of tradition, who mediate between the world of the spirit and the world of matter. Their appearance in the stark world of Antonioni's film is inexplicable until one realizes that they are not meant to appear in *his* kind of film at all. They are Fellini characters, the clowns and fantastically attired circus people, whose joy is gone and whose magical illusion is unmasked as the lie that Antonioni takes it to be. Thomas' collaboration is the sign that he has joined the ranks of the talented perpetrators of illusion, and that he disappears both as person and artist, leaving Antonioni to his lonely search for the truth.

I remarked at the beginning of this paper that literature seems to have been superseded in both the popular and the intellectual imagination by the new visual media. But Antonioni's film makes the point that the recognition in art of human mortality can be evaded but never superseded. His critique of the medium and of its capacity to lie, at the very inception of a new technological era, is reminiscent of the critique of the new printing medium launched by Cervantes at the beginning of this (now dying) linear age. In the second part of *Don Quixote*, Altisidora has a dream which symbolizes the disenchanted view of the new cultural revolution. She describes her dream:

> The truth is, I arrived at the gate of Hell, where something like a dozen devils were playing tennis, all in their breeches and doublets, with their collars trimmed with Flanders lace and with ruffles of the same which served them as cuffs with four inches of arm bare to make their hands look longer. They were holding rackets of fire and

what most astonished me was that instead of balls they used what
looked like books, stuffed with wind and fluff . . .

Technology has been refined to the point that the message has lost
even the physical reality still represented by the book, the word has
turned to image, while sender and receiver stare blankly as though
their transaction at some point still touched the solidarity of the
ground. Their game, in which everyone loses, is one that Antonioni
refuses steadfastly to play. In his own terms, he can hope for no greater
victory.

Synopsis

A successful young photographer returns to his studio after spending the night disguised as a bum in a shelter for down-and-out men. He has been secretly recording the seamy side of London life for a picture book he is creating, but must begin his regular day's work: photographing fashion models.

Later on, while wandering near the tennis courts in a park with his camera, he catches sight of a young woman kissing and embracing a middle-aged man. Intrigued by their odd *pas-de-deux*, the photographer secretly follows and photographs them until he is interrupted by the young woman herself, who tries unsuccessfully to wrest the camera and film from him.

Returning to his studio, the photographer encounters the same girl, who has obviously followed him home. This time she offers sex in exchange for the film, but the photographer deceives her by giving her a blank roll. Alone, his curiosity fully aroused, the photographer develops the shots and enlarges parts of one of them to reveal what looks like a man with a gun concealed in the bushes.

At first the photographer thinks his own presence in the park prevented a murder, but after glancing again at the photographs, he discovers what appears to be a corpse on the ground. He makes a nocturnal visit to the park, where he finds the body of the middle-aged lover —its face wax-like and grotesquely illuminated by the glare from a nearby neon sign.

After returning to his studio, the photographer finds the apartment ransacked and most of the incriminating blow-ups stolen. He then goes to a marijuana party where he tries to convince a friend—the writer who is collaborating with him on his picture book—to go with him to the park to photograph the corpse. The writer is too stoned to understand, and the photographer, frustrated and exhausted, falls asleep.

Early the next morning, the photographer returns to the park. The body is gone, but a group of students, whose faces are painted like clowns and who appeared briefly on the street at the opening of the film, are miming a game of tennis on a nearby tennis court. The photographer joins them and pretends to retrieve their nonexistent ball. Sounds of an actual ball being hit can be heard on the sound track, and, as the camera pulls back into a long overhead shot of the photographer, he suddenly vanishes from the field.

Outline

London Street Scene   *Exterior: Dawn*

A group of students, their faces painted white, noisily drive by in a
jeep. They are returning from a night of celebration during Rag Week.

Thomas, disguised as a bum, emerges from a mission-type shelter
with a bunch of ragged men, his camera concealed in a piece of
wrapping paper [Plate I]. He gets into a Rolls Royce and drives away.

Photographer's Studio   *Interior: Day*

Without changing his clothes, Thomas photographs, in a series of
erotic poses, a famous model (played by Verushka). Both are left exhausted, but sexually unsatisfied [Plate II].

After washing and shaving, Thomas then photographs a group of
female models dressed in chic but outlandish mod clothes, arranging
them in various positions both behind and in front of a collection of
large smoked-glass screens [Plate III].

Painter's Studio   *Interior: Day*

Thomas visits the neighboring studio apartment of a painter and
his wife, where he tries, unsuccessfully, to buy one of the artist's abstract paintings. The painter reveals how, occasionally, he finds in
his paintings something representational to "hold on to" [Plate IV].

Photographer's Studio   *Interior: Day*

Thomas returns to his own studio, where he turns away two teenage
girls seeking to become models.

Antique Shop   *Interior: Day*

Thomas drives to an antique shop that he hopes to buy, but finds it tended by a reticent old man who seems more anxious to keep than sell the merchandise [Plate V].

Park   *Exterior: Day*

Camera in hand, Thomas wanders happily into a nearby park [Plate VI]. After photographing a few pigeons, he comes upon a couple—a young woman and a middle-aged man—alternately walking and embracing. Hiding behind trees and bushes, he photographs them with a telephoto lens [Plate VII].

The woman notices him and tries unsuccessfully to obtain the roll of film. Thomas takes more pictures of her as she runs away.

Antique Shop   *Interior: Day*

Leaving the park, Thomas goes into the antique shop again, where he buys an old airplane propeller from a bored young lady—presumably the store's owner—whose only ambition seems to be to escape from life in London to some remote romantic place like Nepal.

Restaurant   *Interior: Day*

A short while later, Thomas lunches with the writer friend who is providing the commentary for his picture book. He starts to explain how the photographs of the couple in the park will give a peaceful conclusion to the otherwise violent and harsh tone of the book. But their conversation is interrupted by the sight of a mysterious young man momentarily peering into the restaurant at them.

Photographer's Studio   *Interior: Day*

Back at his studio, Thomas finds the girl of the park waiting for him. Her graceful movements appeal to his artist's eye, and he directs her in a series of basic poses [Plate VIII]. She again begs for the roll of film, and offers to go to bed with him in exchange for it, but their lovemaking is interrupted by the delivery of the propeller. Thomas gives the girl a blank roll in exchange for what she alleges is her phone number. Intently curious about the nature of the photographs which upset the girl so much, Thomas develops the roll of film and makes enlargements of some of the prints until they reveal a man in the bushes holding a gun [Plates IX, X, XI].

Thinking he has prevented a murder, Thomas telephones his writer friend to tell him the news, but seems unable to convince him. The two teen-age girls aspiring to be models return and engage Thomas in a nude frolick. From his exhausted position on the floor, he notices the outlines of a corpse in one of the blow-ups on a drying line.

Park   *Exterior: Night*

Thomas goes to the park and finds the corpse of the middle-aged lover staring towards the sky, its face lighted by a nearby neon sign. A click resembling the shutter of a camera frightens the photographer away.

Artist's Apartment   *Interior: Night*

Thomas wanders into the apartment of his neighbors, the painter and his wife, and discovers the couple having intercourse. He remains unnoticed by the husband, but the wife fixes him with an inviting stare.

Photographer's Studio   *Interior: Night*

The photographer returns home to find the incriminating photos stolen. The artist's wife drops by in order to confide in Thomas about her marital unhappiness, but he is only able to talk about the corpse in the park.

Street   *Exterior: Night*

While driving to a party, where he hopes to meet his writer friend, Thomas thinks he sees the girl of the park going into a discothèque.

Discothèque   *Interior: Night*

The girl is nowhere to be seen, but Thomas is diverted by a fracas which occurs when one of the musicians, frustrated by a faulty amplifier, breaks up his electric guitar and throws it into the audience. In the ensuing mad scramble for the prized fragments, Thomas runs away with the largest piece.

Street   *Exterior: Night*

Thomas throws the guitar fragment into the gutter. A puzzled passer-by picks it up, then discards it.

Writer's Apartment   *Interior: Night*

A marijuana party is in progress. Thomas tries to get his doped up host to go to the park with him in order to photograph the body, but the uncomprehending writer refuses. Thomas falls into a bed exhausted and sleeps until early morning.

Park   *Exterior: Dawn*

Returning to the park, Thomas discovers that the corpse has disappeared. As he wanders past the tennis courts, the group of students who appeared briefly at the opening of the film, appear on the scene and begin to mime a tennis match. Thomas is drawn into their world of make-believe when he pretends to recover their imaginary ball.

As the camera pulls far back in a long overhead shot, Thomas seems to dwindle in size against the green field, and then disappears entirely from the screen.

Three Sequences from BLOW-UP:
A Shot Analysis
by KAY HINES

I. PARK-EXTERIOR-DAY

1. *Long shot*—A park. Through the entrance can be seen the antique shop. Thomas slowly approaches the park.

2. *Medium long shot*—On the lush green lawn a heavy woman in work clothes is spearing bits of paper on a stick. Thomas passes by her on his way. He stops—*medium shot*—and looks around him.

3. *Long shot*—He looks out over the expanse of the park, over a tennis court he has passed on his way into the park.

4. *Medium shot*—*The regular sound of balls being hit* back and forth. Thomas takes a picture.

5–6. *Long shot*—He scatters pigeons to photograph them. *The camera follows* one of the soaring birds and *stops* on a group of high-rise buildings in the background.

7. *Long shot*—Thomas strolls back across the lawn and then looks to his left.

8. *Long shot*—A man and woman, hand in hand, scramble up a slope to some bushes. *Birds twitter.*

9. *Semi-long shot*—A path leads up the hill. Thomas bounds up it joyfully [Plate VI]. Then—*medium long shot*—he goes slowly up the steps, stops behind a bush—*medium close-up*—focuses with his camera, and snaps. Then he looks around.

10. *Long shot*—The couple runs laughing across a meadow. She pulls him along with her.

11–13. *Medium long shot*—Thomas stands on one of the paths, then leaps over a green wood railing, crouches behind it among the branches, and shoots—*medium close-up*. He runs—*medium shot to medium long shot*—a little way, crouched down along the fence. *The wind rustles in the trees.*

14. *Reverse angle* on the couple—*long shot*.

15. *Medium long shot*—Thomas follows them cautiously, hides behind a tree, and shoots in rapid succession.

16–21. Thomas, crouching behind a tree with his back to the camera—*medium long shot to long shot*—photographs the two of them as they embrace [Plate VII]. *Oblique long shot tilting down* on Thomas as he creeps to the next tree closer to the couple. The woman glances hesitantly around as though she is looking for something; the two have not yet noticed the photographer. Thomas goes slowly back again and stops once more behind a tree. The man pulls the woman under the trees and they embrace. Thomas heads slowly for the park entrance.

22. *Medium long shot*—Both of them have seen him now. The man, dressed in a light-colored suit, looks at him. The woman (Vanessa Redgrave) dashes after him with long strides. *The camera pans slowly* with her.

23. *Medium long shot*—Thomas runs down the steps, then turns abruptly and photographs the woman, who—*off camera*—is running after him.
   JANE (*off*): "What are you doing?"

24. *Medium long shot*—She comes running down the steps towards Thomas.
   (*On*): "Stop it! Stop it! Give me those pictures. You can't move about people like that."
   She stands beside him agitated and out of breath.
   THOMAS: "Who says I can't? . . . I'm only doing my job." He speaks playfully. "Some people are bullfighters; some people are politicians. I'm a photographer."

25. *Reverse angle* over Thomas' shoulder onto Jane—*medium shot*.
   JANE: "This is a public place. Everyone has the right to be left in peace." *The camera follows* Thomas, who leans against the fence.
   THOMAS: "It's not my fault if there's no peace . . . You know most girls would pay me to photograph them."

26. *Medium shot*—Thomas is standing a few steps above her. She offers to buy the roll of film; he refuses.

He goes back towards the park. Jane looks after him disconcerted.

27. *Medium long shot*—Thomas, strolling across the meadow again, is going to take more photographs. Jane rushes to him.

28. *Medium shot*—She is standing in front of him again. He promises to send her the pictures, but she lunges for the camera. He hangs on to it.

29–35. Jane tries to snatch the camera away from him—*medium shot, angle down from above*—and drops to her knees. She bites his hand. He shouts at her.

Medium close-up—Thomas has torn the camera away with a hard yank and Jane, on her knees, dazed and on the verge of hysterics, brushes the hair back from her face and stares at him desperately. THOMAS gazes at her coolly: "Don't let's spoil everything. We've only just met."

Jane stands up slowly and takes a few steps back. She draws a deep breath and announces defiantly that they don't know each other.

36. *Medium shot to medium long shot*—Thomas takes a lens shade and mounts it on his camera again. Jane looks back across the meadow seeming to search for something, and runs away.

37. *Long shot*—She is running across the meadow.

38. *Medium shot to medium long shot*—Thomas shoots after her.

39. *Long shot*—Jane stops by a bush and then runs on. The man has disappeared, but an indistinct shape can be seen on the ground near the bush.

II. Studio-Interior-Day

(Jane has just left)

1. *Medium long shot*—Thomas is standing up on the stairs, the slip of paper with her number in his hand. He stares after her and then goes slowly back into the studio.

2. *Medium shot*—He pours himself a drink, sits down, and slaps his thigh impatiently. He stands up indecisively, goes slowly towards the door, and then suddenly . . .

3. *Medium shot*—. . . starts running along the passage to the dark room. He has pulled on his shirt on the way. In the dark room, he arranges his materials and closes the lavender sliding door. *The*

camera, remaining outside, pans to a light by the door. It flashes on red.

4–8. *Medium close-up*—From an automatic developing cabinet Thomas takes two strips of film [Plate IX]. The light outside goes off.

Thomas—*medium shot*—goes into the next room and closes a yellow sliding door. Again a red light beside it flashes on. Inside Thomas has laid the cut pieces of film strip over the light box and examines them closely with a magnifying glass. His eye stops on one of the images. He makes an enlargement of this shot in the dim yellowish light of the room.

9. *Medium long shot, later medium shot*—He goes along the gallery carrying the print still wet.

10. *Medium long shot*—View over the couch across to two photos hanging there and showing scenes from the park (black and white).

11. *Medium long shot*—Thomas lies on the couch smoking, then sits up staring at the photographs.

12. *Close-up*—*The camera pans back and forth* between the two pictures. They show Jane and the man.

13. Thomas bends intently over the pictures. *The camera pans behind* them. His shadow shows through on the back side. Something seems to have caught his attention.

14–17. *Medium close-up*—He stands in front of the pictures, goes away, and returns with another print, an enlargement of Jane embracing the man. Jane is looking off to the right of the picture. With the help of the other pictures, where he traces her line of vision with his finger, he tries to figure out what she is looking at. Then he shrugs his shoulders.

18. *Medium shot to medium long shot*—*The camera follows* him between the pictures as he pours himself a drink and then sits down, his eyes glued pensively to the photographs. *Rythmical music begins to play* again.

19. *Extreme close-up*—He sets the glass down and picks up the magnifying glass. Now—*medium close-up*—*the camera follows* him as he scrutinizes one of the pictures intently with the magnifying glass. Suddenly his movements quicken. He seems to have discovered something. With a grease pencil he draws a small square on the photograph and takes it away [Plate X]. *The music has stopped.*

20. *Close-up*—The enlargement. Thomas stands pensively in front of it [Plate XI]. Behind a fence the indistinct form of a man can be made out in the bushes.

21. *Close-up—The camera pans back and forth* on the photographs. Now it seems that the face of the man can be seen more clearly.

22. *Medium close-up—*Thomas ponders tensely.

23. *Medium shot—*In the dark room he prepares another enlargement.

24. *Medium shot—*He mounts several photos on a white sheet.

25. *Close-up—The camera travels* over the photographs: several scenes between the girl and the man. Thomas stands thoughtfully in front of them and again studies the different angles.

26. *Medium long shot—*He seems to have given up. Then he remembers the slip of paper with the phone number. He rushes to the phone and dials. It is obviously not Jane's number. He slams down the receiver and crumples the slip of paper.

27. *Medium close-up—*He ponders the photos again. Suddenly an idea comes to him. He dashes through the studio. *The camera pans* after him.

28. *Medium close-up to close-up—*In the dark room he makes still another enlargement, and even as it is being developed he looks curiously at the print.

29–30. *Medium shot—*In the studio he hangs the print beside the others. He has meanwhile hung up the pictures on three sides around him. He studies the series.

31–35. *Close-up—*The individual shots, the scenes of the two lovers, *are cut one after the other. There is the sound of wind* as it was there in the park. *The camera pans* on the man in the bushes.

36. *Close-up—*The man in the bushes. His hand can be made out. He is holding something.

37. *Extreme close-up—*The outline of a pistol can be distinguished among the branches.

38. *Close-up—*Jane, just embraced by the man. Now it is obvious that she is looking at the man in the bushes.

39–45. More scenes, in black and white, of the park. Jane in the meantime has spotted the photographer, runs towards him, and later runs back into the park. The entire sequence of events from the park is concentrated in a few photos.

46. *Medium close-up—*Thomas stands in front of them reflecting and then goes to the telephone. *The wind's rustling has stopped.* THOMAS: "Ron? . . . Something fantastic's happened! Those photos in the park! Fantastic! Somebody was trying to kill somebody else. I saved his life. . . . What makes it so fantastic . . ."

The door bell rings. Thomas asks Ron to hold on while he answers the door.

47. *Close-up*—He glances back at the photos, and then . . .

48. *Medium long shot*—. . . goes to the door, hesitates, and steps behind it, slowly pushing the handle down. At first a green bottom and lavender legs jump back. Then Jenny looks in and Thomas bursts out laughing.

III. PARK-EXTERIOR-NIGHT

1-2. *Long shot*—Thomas parks his car in front of the entrance and goes into the park. It is windy. *The camera pans* after him and *stops* on a large neon sign which sparsely illuminates the park.

3-5. He goes up the steps and slowly into the park. *The camera pans* after him, *catching* him—*now in long shot*—as he runs hesitatingly across the lawn.

6. *Medium shot*—*The camera dollies* after Thomas as he goes over to a bush, and *then tilts down* to the ground. A face gleams in the light.

7. *Medium shot*—Thomas goes slowly, step by step, until he is standing by the dead man. He bends over him. He can be recognized as the man in the light-colored suit who was romping over the lawn with Jane.

8. *Medium close-up*—Thomas swallows.

9. *Medium close-up*—*Reverse angle* onto the dead man. His open eyes stare upwards.

10. *Medium shot*—Thomas stands up slowly.

11. *Medium close-up*—He looks around him.

12. *Medium long shot*—Then he goes, at first slowly and then faster, his white trousers reflecting the light of the electric sign. In the distance he looks around him once more.

Filmography

I. As COLLABORATOR

As Assistant Director:

I Due Foscari, directed by Enrico Fulchignoni (1942)
Les visiteurs du soir, directed by Marcel Carné (1942)

As Co-Scenarist:

I Due Foscari, co-authored by G. Campanile Mancinie, Mino Doletti, Enrico Fulchignoni. Directed by Enrico Fulchignoni (1942).

Un pilota ritorna, co-authored by Rosario Leone, Ugo Betti, Massimo Mida, Gherardo Gherardi. Directed by Roberto Rossillini (1942).

Caccia Tragica, co-authored by Giuseppe de Santis, Carlo Lizzani, Cesare Zavattini, Corrado Alvaro, Umberto Barbaro, Tullio Pinelli. Directed by Giuseppe de Santis (1947).

Lo Sceicco Bianco, co-authored by Federico Fellini and Tullio Pinelli. Directed by Federico Fellini (1952).

II. As DIRECTOR

Documentaries and Shorts

Gente del Po (1947)
Production company. I.C.E.T.—Carpi
Photographer: Piero Portalupi
Composer: Mario Labroca

N. U. (Nettezza Urbana) (1948)
Production company: Lux Film
Photographer: Giovanni Ventimiglia
Composers: Jazz arrangement by Giovanni Fusco and Prelude by J. S. Bach.

L'Amorosa Menzogna (1949)
    Production company: Fortuna Film
    Photographer: Renato del Frate
    Composer: Giovanni Fusco

Superstizione (1949)
    Production company: I.C.E.T.—Carpi
    Photographer: Giovanni Ventimiglia
    Composer: Giovanni Fusco

La Funivia del Faloria (1950)
    Production company: Teo Usuelli
    Photographer: Goffredo Bellisario and Ghedina
    Composer: Teo Usuelli

Sette Canne, Un Vestito (1949)
    Production company: I.C.E.T.—Carpi
    Photographer: Giovanni Ventimiglia
    Composers: various, from recordings

La Villa dei Mostri (1950)
    Production company: Filmus
    Photographer: Giovanni de Paoli
    Composer: Giovanni Fusco

Uomini in piu (1955)
    Production: C.I.M.E.

Feature Films

Cronaca di un amore (1950)
    Production company: Franco Villani and Stefano Caretta
        for Villani Films
    Photographer: Enzo Serafin
    Screenwriters: Michelangelo Antonioni, Danièle d'Anza, Silvio
        Giovaninetti, Francesco Maselli, Piero Tellini
    Composer: Giovanni Fusco
    Actors: Lucia Bose, Massimo Girotti, Ferdinando Sarmi, Gino
        Rossi, Marika Rowsky, Rosa Mirafiore, Rubi d'Alma

I Vinti (1952)
    Production company: Film-Constellazione, S.G.C.
    Photographer: Enzo Serafin
    Screenwriters: Michelangelo Antonioni, Suso Cecchi d'Amico,
        Diego Fabbri, Turi Valile
    Composer: Giovanni Fusco
    Actors:
        Italian episode: Anna Maria Ferrero, Franco Interlenghi,

Eduardo Cianelli, Evi Maltagliati, Umberto Sparado, Gastone Renzelli

English episode: Peter Reynolds, Patrick Barr, Fay Compton, Eileen Moore

French episode: Henry Poirier, André Jacques, Jean-Pierre Mocky, Etchika Choureau, Annie Noël

La Signora senza Camelie (1953)

Production company: Domenico Forges Davanzati for E.N.I.C.

Photographer: Enzo Serafin

Screenwriters: Michelangelo Antonioni, Suso Cecchi d'Amico, Francesco Maselli, P. M. Pasinetti

Composer: Giovanni Fusco

Actors: Lucia Bose, Andrea Cecchi, Gino Cervi, Ivan Desny, Alain Cuny, Monica Clay, Anna Carena, Enrico Glori

Tentato suicido—an episode in *L'Amore in Città* (1953)

Production company: Faro Film

Photographer: Gianni di Venanzo

Screenwriters: Michelangelo Antonioni, Cesare Zavattini, Aldo Buzzi, Luigi Chiarini, Luigi Malerba, Tullio Pinelli, Vittorio Veltroni

Composer: Mario Nascimbene

Actors: The actual survivors of the events shown in the film

Le Amiche (1955)

Production company: Trionfalcine

Photographer: Gianni di Venanzo

Screenwriters: Michelangelo Antonioni, Suso Cecchi d'Amico, Alba de Cespedes

Composer: Giovanni Fusco

Actors: Eleonora Rossi Drago, Valentina Cortese, Gabriele Ferzetti, Franco Fabrizi, Ettore Manni, Madeleine Fischer, Yvonne Furneaux, Anna Maria Pancani

Il Grido (1957)

Production company: Franco Cancellieri for S.P.A. Cinematografica, in collaboration with Robert Alexander Productions of New York

Photographer: Gianni di Venanzo

Screenwriters: Michelangelo Antonioni, Elio Gartolini, Ennio di Concini

Composer: Giovanni Fusco

Actors: Steve Cochran, Alida Valli, Dorian Gray, Betsy Blair, Lynn Shaw, Gabriella Pallotto, Gaetano Matteucci, Guerrino Campanili, Pina Boldrini

L'Avventura (1960)

Production company: A Cino Del Duca Co-Production: Produzioni Cinematografiche Europee (Rome) and Société Cinématographique Lyre (Paris)
Photographer: Aldo Scavarda
Screenwriters: Michelangelo Antonioni, Elio Bartolini, Tonino Guerra
Composer: Giovanni Fusco
Actors: Gabriele Ferzetti, Monica Vitti, Lea Massari, Dominique Blanchar, Renzo Ricci, James Addams, Dorothy de Poliolo, Lelio Luttazzi, Giovanni Petrucci, Esmeralda Ruspoli, Enrico Bologna, Franco Cimino, Giovanni Danesi, Rita Mole, Renato Pinciroli, Angelo Tommasi di Lampedusa, Vincenzo Tranchina

La Notte (1960)

Production companies: Emmanuel Cassuto, for Nepi-Film (Rome), Silva-Film (Rome) and Sofitedip (Paris)
Photographer: Gianni di Venanzo
Screenwriters: Michelangelo Antonioni, Ennio Flaiano, Tonino Guerra
Composer: Giorgio Gaslini
Actors: Jeanne Moreau, Marcello Mastroianni, Monica Vitti, Bernhard Wicki

L'Eclisse (1961)

Production company: Robert and Raymond Hakim
Photographer: Gianni di Venanzo
Screenwriters: Michelangelo Antonioni, Tonino Guerra, Elio Bartolini, Ottiero Ottieri
Composer: Giovanni Fusco
Actors: Alain Delon, Monica Vitti, Francisco Rabal, Louis Seigner, Lilla Brignone, Rossana Rory, Mirella Ricciardi

Deserto rosso (1964)

Production company: Antonio Cervi for Film Duemila, Cinematografica Federiz (Rome), Francoriz (Paris)
Photographer: Carlo di Palma
Screenwriters: Michelangelo Antonioni and Tonino Guerra
Composers: Giovanni Fusco and Vittorio Gelmetti
Actors: Monica Vitti, Richard Harris, Carlo Chionetti, Xenia Valderi, Rita Renoir, Aldo Grotti, Giuliano Missirini, Lili Rheims, Valerio Bartoleschi, Emanuela Paola Carboni, Bruno Borghi, Beppe Conti, Giulio Cotignoli, Giovanni Lolli, Hiram Mino Madonia, Arturo Parmiani, Carla Ravasi, Ivo Cherpiani, Bruno Scipioni

Prefazione—an episode from *I Tre volti* (1965)
> Production company: Dino de Laurentiis Cinematografica
> Photographer: Carlo di Palma
> Screenwriter: Piero Tosi
> Composer: Piero Piccioni
> Actors: Soraya, Ivano Davoli, Giorgio Sartarelli, Piero Tosi, Dino De Laurentiis, Alfredo De Laurentiis, Ralph Serpe

Blow-Up (1966)
> Production company: Bridge Films (Carlo Ponti) for Metro-Goldwyn-Mayer
> Photographer: Carlo di Palma
> Screenwriters: Michelangelo Antonioni and Tonino Guerra
> Composer: Herbert Hancock
> Actors: David Hemmings, Vanessa Redgrave, Sarah Miles, Peter Bowles, Verushka, Jill Kennington, Peggy Moffitt, Rosaleen Murray, Ann Norman, Melanie Hampshire, Jane Birkin, Gillian Hills, Harry Hutchinson, John Castle.

Zabriskie Point (1969)
> Production company: Carlo Ponti for Metro-Goldwyn-Mayer
> Photographer: Alfio Cortini
> Screenwriter: Michelangelo Antonioni
> Actors: Rod Taylor, Diana Halprin, Mark Frechette

Bibliography

BOOKS

Bernardini, Aldo, *Michelangelo Antonioni da "Gente del Po" a "Blow-Up."* Milan: Edizioni 17, 1967. (In Italian only)

Cameron, Ian and Robin Wood, *Antonioni.* New York: Praeger, 1968.

Cowie, Peter. *Antonioni, Bergman, Resnais.* London: The Tantivy Press, 1963.

Huss, Roy and Norman Silverstein, *The Film Experience.* New York: Harper & Row, 1968. (References to Antonioni *passim*)

Leprohon, Pierre, *Michelangelo Antonioni,* trans. Scot Sullivan. New York: Simon and Schuster, 1963.

————, *Michelangelo Antonioni,* 4th edition. Paris: Editions Seghers, 1969. (A completely revised version of the above, with new material. In French only.)

Strick, Philip. *Antonioni.* Loughton: Motion Pictures Publications, 1963.

ARTICLES

Garis, Robert, "Watching Antonioni," *Commentary* 43 (April 1967): 86–89. (Reply by P. Warshow, with rejoinder by Garis, *Commentary* 44 [August 1967]: 14–17.)

Goldstein, Richard, "The Screw-Up," *Village Voice,* December 29, 1966, p. 21.

Hernacki, Thomas, "Michelangelo Antonioni and the Imagery of Disintegration," *Film Heritage* 5 (Spring 1970): 13–21.

Kael, Pauline, "Tourist in the City of Youth," *Kiss, Kiss, Bang, Bang.* Boston: Atlantic-Little, Brown and Co., 1967, pp. 31–37.

Lefèvre, Raymond, "Blow-Up," *Image et Son,* November 1967, pp. 111–15.

Sherman, William David, "Antonioni in the Psychedelic Sixties," *Landscape of Contemporary Cinema.* Buffalo: Buffalo Spectrum Press, 1967.

INTERVIEWS

Godard, Jean-Luc, "The Art of the Director: Godard Interviews Antonioni," *Cahiers du Cinéma in English,* January 1966, pp. 19–30. (Reprinted in T. J. Ross, ed., *Film and the Liberal Arts* [New York: Holt, Rinehart and Winston, 1970].)

Liber, Nadine, "Antonioni Talks About His Work," *Life,* January 27, 1967, pp. 66–67.

Reed, Rex, "Interview with Antonioni," *New York Times,* sec. II, Sunday, January 1, 1967, p. 7. (Letter by Antonioni criticizing this interview, *New York Times* sec. II, Sunday, January 15, 1967, p. 17.)

Samuels, Charles Thomas, "Interview with Antonioni" (Part I), *Vogue* 155 (March 15, 1970): 96–97.

———, "Interview with Antonioni" (Part II), *Film Heritage* 5 (Spring 1970): 1–12.

Watts, Stephen, "London, In and Out of Focus," *New York Times,* sec. II, Sunday, July 31, 1966, p. 7.

SCRIPTS AND SCREENPLAYS FOR BLOW-UP

In English: *Blow-Up.* New York: Simon and Schuster, forthcoming.
In Italian: *Blow-Up.* Turin: Giulio Einaudi, 1968.
In German: *"Blow-Up," Film* 5 (June 1967): 41–51.
In Spanish: *Blow-Up, las Amigas, e Grito, La Aventura.* Madrid: Alianza Editorial, 1968.
In Swedish: *Blow-Up.* Stockholm: Norstedts, 1967.

APPENDIX

BLOW-UP

by JULIO CORTÁZAR

It'll never be known how this has to be told, in the first person or
in the second, using the third person plural or continually inventing
modes that will serve for nothing. If one might say: I will see the
moon rose, or: we hurt me at the back of my eyes, and especially: you
the blond woman was the clouds that race before my your his our
yours their faces. What the hell.

Seated ready to tell it, if one might go to drink a bock over there,
and the typewriter continue by itself (because I use the machine),
that would be perfection. And that's not just a manner of speaking.
Perfection, yes, because here is the aperture which must be counted
also as a machine (of another sort, a Contax 1.1.2) and it is possible
that one machine may know more about another machine than I, you,
she—the blond—and the clouds. But I have the dumb luck to know
that if I go this Remington will sit turned to stone on top of the table
with the air of being twice as quiet that mobile things have when they
are not moving. So, I have to write. One of us all has to write, if this
is going to get told. Better that it be me who am dead, for I'm less
compromised than the rest; I who see only the clouds and can think
without being distracted, write without being distracted (there goes
another, with a grey edge) and remember without being distracted, I
who am dead (and I'm alive, I'm not trying to fool anybody, you'll see
when we get to the moment, because I have to begin some way and
I've begun with this period, the last one back, the one at the beginning,
which in the end is the best of the periods when you want to tell something).

All of a sudden I wonder why I have to tell this, but if one begins

From Julio Cortázar, End of the Game and Other Stories, *trans. by
Paul Blackburn (New York: Random House, Inc., 1967). Copyright* ©
*1963, 1967 by Random House, Inc. Reprinted by permission of Pantheon
Books, a division of Random House, Inc., and Paul Blackburn.*

to wonder why he does all he does do, if one wonders why he accepts an invitation to lunch (now a pigeon's flying by and it seems to me a sparrow), or why when someone has told us a good joke immediately there starts up something like a tickling in the stomach and we are not at peace until we've gone into the office across the hall and told the joke over again; then it feels good immediately, one is fine, happy, and can get back to work. For I imagine that no one has explained this, that really the best thing is to put aside all decorum and tell it, because, after all's done, nobody is ashamed of breathing or of putting on his shoes; they're things that you do, and when something weird happens, when you find a spider in your shoe or if you take a breath and feel like a broken window, then you have to tell what's happening, tell it to the guys at the office or to the doctor. Oh, doctor, every time I take a breath . . . Always tell it, always get rid of that tickle in the stomach that bothers you.

And now that we're finally going to tell it, let's put things a little bit in order, we'd be walking down the staircase in this house as far as Sunday, November 7, just a month back. One goes down five floors and stands then in the Sunday in the sun one would not have suspected of Paris in November, with a large appetite to walk around, to see things, to take photos (because we were photographers, I'm a photographer). I know that the most difficult thing is going to be finding a way to tell it, and I'm not afraid of repeating myself. It's going to be difficult because nobody really knows who it is telling it, if I am I or what actually occurred or what I'm seeing (clouds, and once in a while a pigeon) or if, simply, I'm telling a truth which is only my truth, and then is the truth only for my stomach, for this impulse to go running out and to finish up in some manner with, this, whatever it is.

We're going to tell it slowly, what happens in the middle of what I'm writing is coming already. If they replace me, if, so soon, I don't know what to say, if the clouds stop coming and something else starts (because it's impossible that this keep coming, clouds passing continually and occasionally a pigeon), if something out of all this . . . And after the "if" what am I going to put if I'm going to close the sentence structure correctly? But if I begin to ask questions, I'll never tell anything, maybe to tell would be like an answer, at least for someone who's reading it.

Roberto Michel, French-Chilean, translator and in his spare time an amateur photographer, left number 11, rue Monsieur-le-Prince Sunday November 7 of the current year (now there're two small ones passing, with silver linings). He had spent three weeks working on the French version of a treatise on challenges and appeals by José

Norberto Allende, professor at the University of Santiago. It's rare that there's wind in Paris, and even less seldom a wind like this that swirled around corners and rose up to whip at old wooden venetian blinds behind which astonished ladies commented variously on how unreliable the weather had been these last few years. But the sun was out also, riding the wind and friend of the cats, so there was nothing that would keep me from taking a walk along the docks of the Seine and taking photos of the Conservatoire and Sainte-Chapelle. It was hardly ten o'clock, and I figured that by eleven the light would be good, the best you can get in the fall; to kill some time I detoured around by the Isle Saint-Louis and started to walk along the quai d'Anjou, I stared for a bit at the hôtel de Lauzun, I recited bits from Apollinaire which always get into my head whenever I pass in front of the hôtel de Lauzun (and at that I ought to be remembering the other poet, but Michel is an obstinate beggar), and when the wind stopped all at once and the sun came out at least twice as hard (I mean warmer, but really it's the same thing), I sat down on the parapet and felt terribly happy in the Sunday morning.

One of the many ways of contesting level-zero, and one of the best, is to take photographs, an activity in which one should start becoming an adept very early in life, teach it to children since it requires discipline, aesthetic education, a good eye and steady fingers. I'm not talking about waylaying the lie like any old reporter, snapping the stupid silhouette of the VIP leaving number 10 Downing Street, but in all ways when one is walking about with a camera, one has almost a duty to be attentive, to not lose that abrupt and happy rebound of sun's rays off an old stone, or the pigtails-flying run of a small girl going home with a loaf of bread or a bottle of milk. Michel knew that the photographer always worked as a permutation of his personal way of seeing the world as other than the camera insidiously imposed upon it (now a large cloud is going by, almost black), but he lacked no confidence in himself, knowing that he had only to go out without the Contax to recover the keynote of distraction, the sight without a frame around it, light without the diaphragm aperture or 1/250 sec. Right now (what a word, *now*, what a dumb lie) I was able to sit quietly on the railing overlooking the river watching the red and black motorboats passing below without it occurring to me to think photographically of the scenes, nothing more than letting myself go in the letting go of objects, running immobile in the stream of time. And then the wind was not blowing.

After, I wandered down the quai de Bourbon until getting to the end of the isle where the intimate square was (intimate because it was small, not that it was hidden, it offered its whole breast to the river and the sky), I enjoyed it, a lot. Nothing there but a couple and, of course, pigeons; maybe even some of those which are flying past now so that I'm seeing them. A leap up and I settled on the wall, and let myself turn about and be caught and fixed by the sun, giving it my face and ears and hands (I kept my gloves in my pocket). I had no desire to shoot pictures, and lit a cigarette to be doing something; I think it was that moment when the match was about to touch the tobacco that I saw the young boy for the first time.

What I'd thought was a couple seemed much more now a boy with his mother, although at the same time I realized that it was not a kid and his mother, and that it was a couple in the sense that we always allegate to couples when we see them leaning up against the parapets or embracing on the benches in the squares. As I had nothing else to do, I had more than enough time to wonder why the boy was so nervous, like a young colt or a hare, sticking his hands into his pockets, taking them out immediately, one after the other, running his fingers through his hair, changing his stance, and especially why was he afraid, well, you could guess that from every gesture, a fear suffocated by his shyness, an impulse to step backwards which he telegraphed, his body standing as if it were on the edge of flight, holding itself back in a final, pitiful decorum.

All this was so clear, ten feet away—and we were alone against the parapet at the tip of the island—that at the beginning the boy's fright didn't let me see the blond very well. Now, thinking back on it, I see her much better at that first second when I read her face (she'd turned around suddenly, swinging like a metal weathercock, and the eyes, the eyes were there), when I vaguely understood what might have been occurring to the boy and figured it would be worth the trouble to stay and watch (the wind was blowing their words away and they were speaking in a low murmur). I think that I know how to look, if it's something I know, and also that every looking oozes with mendacity, because it's that which expels us furthest outside ourselves, without the least guarantee, whereas to smell, or (but Michel rambles on to himself easily enough, there's no need to let him harangue on this way). In any case, if the likely inaccuracy can be seen beforehand, it becomes possible again to look; perhaps it suffices to choose between looking and the reality looked at, to strip things of all their unnecessary clothing. And surely all that is difficult besides.

As for the boy I remember the image before his actual body (that will clear itself up later), while now I am sure that I remember the woman's body much better than the image. She was thin and willowy, two unfair words to describe what she was, and was wearing an almost-black fur coat, almost long, almost handsome. All the morning's wind (now it was hardly a breeze and it wasn't cold) had blown through her blond hair which pared away her white, bleak face—two unfair words—and put the world at her feet and horribly alone in front of her dark eyes, her eyes fell on things like two eagles, two leaps into nothingness, two puffs of green slime. I'm not describing anything, it's more a matter of trying to understand it. And I said two puffs of green slime.

Let's be fair, the boy was well enough dressed and was sporting yellow gloves which I would have sworn belonged to his older brother, a student of law or sociology; it was pleasant to see the fingers of the gloves sticking out of his jacket pocket. For a long time I didn't see his face, barely a profile, not stupid—a terrified bird, a Fra Filippo angel, rice pudding with milk—and the back of an adolescent who wants to take up judo and has had a scuffle or two in defense of an idea or his sister. Turning fourteen, perhaps fifteen, one would guess that he was dressed and fed by his parents but without a nickel in his pocket, having to debate with his buddies before making up his mind to buy a coffee, a cognac, a pack of cigarettes. He'd walk through the streets thinking of the girls in his class, about how good it would be to go to the movies and see the latest film, or to buy novels or neckties or bottles of liquor with green and white labels on them. At home (it would be a respectable home, lunch at noon and romantic landscapes on the walls, with a dark entryway and a mahogany umbrella stand inside the door) there'd be the slow rain of time, for studying, for being mama's hope, for looking like dad, for writing to his aunt in Avignon. So that there was a lot of walking the streets, the whole of the river for him (but without a nickel) and the mysterious city of fifteen-year-olds with its signs in doorways, its terrifying cats, a paper of fried potatoes for thirty francs, the pornographic magazine folded four ways, a solitude like the emptiness of his pockets, the eagerness for so much that was incomprehensible but illumined by a total love, by the availability analogous to the wind and the streets.

This biography was of the boy and of any boy whatsoever, but this particular one now, you could see he was insular, surrounded solely by the blond's presence as she continued talking with him. (I'm tired of insisting, but two long ragged ones just went by. That morning I don't think I looked at the sky once, because what was happening with the boy and the woman appeared so soon I could do nothing but look at them and wait, look at them and . . .) To cut it short, the boy was agitated and one could guess without too much trouble what had just occurred a few minutes before, at most half-an-hour. The boy had come onto the tip of the island, seen the woman and thought her marvelous. The woman was waiting for that because she was there waiting for that, or maybe the boy arrived before her and she saw him from one of the balconies or from a car and got out to meet him, starting the conversation with whatever, from the beginning she was sure that he was going to be afraid and want to run off, and that, naturally, he'd stay, stiff and sullen, pretending experience and the pleasure of the adventure. The rest was easy because it was happening ten feet away from me, and anyone could have gauged the stages of the game, the derisive, competitive fencing; its major attraction was not that it was happening but in foreseeing its denouement. The boy would try to end it by pretending a date, an obligation, whatever, and would go stumbling off disconcerted, wishing he were walking with some assurance, but naked under the mocking glance which would follow him until he was out of sight. Or rather, he would stay there, fascinated or simply incapable of taking the initiative, and the woman would begin to touch his face gently, muss his hair, still talking to him voicelessly, and soon would take him by the arm to lead him off, unless he, with an uneasiness beginning to tinge the edge of desire, even his stake in the adventure, would rouse himself to put his arm around her waist and to kiss her. Any of this could have happened, though it did not, and perversely Michel waited, sitting on the railing, making the settings almost without looking at the camera, ready to take a picturesque shot of a corner of the island with an uncommon couple talking and looking at one another.

Strange how the scene (almost nothing: two figures there mismatched in their youth) was taking on a disquieting aura. I thought it was I imposing it, and that my photo, if I shot it, would reconstitute things in their true stupidity. I would have liked to know what he was thinking, a man in a grey hat sitting at the wheel of a car parked on the dock which led up to the footbridge, and whether he was reading the paper or asleep. I had just discovered him because people inside a parked car have a tendency to disappear, they get lost in that wretched, private cage stripped of the beauty that motion and danger give it. And nevertheless, the car had been there the whole time, forming part (or deforming that part) of the isle. A car: like saying a lighted streetlamp, a park bench. Never like saying wind, sunlight, those elements always new to the skin and the eyes, and also the boy and the woman, unique, put there to change the island, to show it to me in another way. Finally, it may have been that the man with the newspaper also became aware of what was happening and would, like me, feel that malicious sensation of waiting for everything to happen. Now the woman had swung around smoothly, putting the young boy between herself and the wall, I saw them almost in profile, and he was taller, though not much taller, and yet she dominated him, it seemed like she was hovering over him (her laugh, all at once, a whip of feathers), crushing him just by being there, smiling, one hand taking a stroll through the air. Why wait any longer? Aperture at sixteen, a sighting which would not include the horrible black car, but yes, that tree, necessary to break up too much grey space . . .

I raised the camera, pretended to study a focus which did not include them, and waited and watched closely, sure that I would finally catch the revealing expression, one that would sum it all up, life that is rhythmed by movement but which a stiff image destroys, taking time in cross section, if we do not choose the essential imperceptible fraction of it. I did not have to wait long. The woman was getting on with the job of handcuffing the boy smoothly, stripping from him what was left of his freedom a hair at a time, in an incredibly slow and delicious torture. I imagined the possible endings (now a small fluffy cloud appears, almost alone in the sky), I saw their arrival at the house (a basement apartment probably, which she would have filled with large cushions and cats) and conjectured the boy's terror and his desperate decision to play it cool and to be led off pretending there was nothing new in it for him. Closing my eyes, if I did in fact close my eyes, I set the scene: the teasing kisses, the woman mildly repelling the hands which were trying to undress her, like in novels, on a bed that would have a lilac-colored comforter, on the other hand she taking off his clothes, plainly mother and son under a milky yellow light, and everything would end up as usual, perhaps, but maybe everything would go otherwise, and the initiation of the adolescent would not happen, she would not let it happen, after a long prologue wherein the awkwardnesses, the exasperating caresses, the running of hands over bodies would be resolved in who knows what, in a separate and solitary pleasure, in a petulant denial mixed with the art of tiring and disconcerting so much poor innocence. It might go like that, it might very well go like that; that woman was not looking for the boy as a lover, and at the same time she was dominating him toward some end impossible to understand if you do not imagine it as a cruel game, the desire to desire without satisfaction, to excite herself for someone else, someone who in no way could be that kid.

Michel is guilty of making literature, of indulging in fabricated unrealities. Nothing pleases him more than to imagine exceptions to the rule, individuals outside the species, not-always-repugnant monsters. But that woman invited speculation, perhaps giving clues enough for the fantasy to hit the bullseye. Before she left, and now that she would fill my imaginings for several days, for I'm given to ruminating, I decided not to lose a moment more. I got it all into the view-finder (with the tree, the railing, the eleven-o'clock sun) and took the shot. In time to realize that they both had noticed and stood there looking at me, the boy surprised and as though questioning, but she was ir-

ritated, her face and body flat-footedly hostile, feeling robbed, ig-
nominiously recorded on a small chemical image.

I might be able to tell it in much greater detail but it's not worth
the trouble. The woman said that no one had the right to take a picture without permission, and demanded that I hand her over the film.
All this in a dry, clear voice with a good Parisian accent, which rose in
color and tone with every phrase. For my part, it hardly mattered
whether she got the roll of film or not, but anyone who knows me will
tell you, if you want anything from me, ask nicely. With the result that
I restricted myself to formulating the opinion that not only was photography in public places not prohibited, but it was looked upon with decided favor, both private and official. And while that was getting said, I
noticed on the sly how the boy was falling back, sort of actively backing
up though without moving, and all at once (it seemed almost incredible) he turned and broke into a run, the poor kid, thinking that he was
walking off and in fact in full flight, running past the side of the car,
disappearing like a gossamer filament of angel-spit in the morning air.

But filaments of angel-spittle are also called devil-spit, and Michel
had to endure rather particular curses, to hear himself called meddler
and imbecile, taking great pains meanwhile to smile and to abate with
simple movements of his head such a hard sell. As I was beginning to
get tired, I heard the car door slam. The man in the grey hat was there,
looking at us. It was only at that point that I realized he was playing a
part in the comedy.

He began to walk toward us, carrying in his hand the paper he had
been pretending to read. What I remember best is the grimace that
twisted his mouth askew, it covered his face with wrinkles, changed
somewhat both in location and shape because his lips trembled and the
grimace went from one side of his mouth to the other as though it were
on wheels, independent and involuntary. But the rest stayed fixed, a
flour-powdered clown or bloodless man, dull dry skin, eyes deepset, the
nostrils black and prominently visible, blacker than the eyebrows or
hair or the black necktie. Walking cautiously as though the pavement
hurt his feet; I saw patent-leather shoes with such thin soles that he
must have felt every roughness in the pavement. I don't know why I
got down off the railing, nor very well why I decided to not give them
the photo, to refuse that demand in which I guessed at their fear and
cowardice. The clown and the woman consulted one another in silence:
we made a perfect and unbearable triangle, something I felt compelled
to break with a crack of a whip. I laughed in their faces and began to
walk off, a little more slowly, I imagine, than the boy. At the level of
the first houses, beside the iron footbridge, I turned around to look
at them. They were not moving, but the man had dropped his news-

paper; it seemed to me that the woman, her back to the parapet, ran her hands over the stone with the classical and absurd gesture of someone pursued looking for a way out.

What happened after that happened here, almost just now, in a room on the fifth floor. Several days went by before Michel developed the photos he'd taken on Sunday; his shots of the Conservatoire and of Sainte-Chapelle were all they should be. Then he found two or three proof-shots he'd forgotten, a poor attempt to catch a cat perched astonishingly on the roof of a rambling public urinal, and also the shot of the blond and the kid. The negative was so good that he made an enlargement; the enlargement was so good that he made one very much larger, almost the size of a poster. It did not occur to him (now one wonders and wonders) that only the shots of the Conservatoire were worth so much work. Of the whole series, the snap-shot of the tip of the island was the only one which interested him; he tacked up the enlargement on one wall of the room, and the first day he spent some time looking at it and remembering, that gloomy operation of comparing the memory with the gone reality; a frozen memory, like any photo, where nothing is missing, not even, and especially, nothingness, the true solidifier of the scene. There was the woman, there was the boy, the tree rigid above their heads, the sky as sharp as the stone of the parapet, clouds and stones melded into a single substance and inseparable (now one with sharp edges is going by, like a thunderhead). The first two days I accepted what I had done, from the photo itself to the enlargement on the wall, and I didn't even question that every once in a while I would interrupt my translation of José Norberto Allende's treatise to encounter once more the woman's face, the dark splotches on the railing. I'm such a jerk; it had never occurred to me that when we look at a photo from the front, the eyes reproduce exactly the position and the vision of the lens; it's these things that are taken for granted and it never occurs to anyone to think about them. From my chair, with the typewriter directly in front of me, I looked at the photo ten feet away, and then it occurred to me that I had hung it exactly at the point of view of the lens. It looked very good that way; no doubt, it was the best way to appreciate a photo, though the angle from the diagonal doubtless has its pleasures and might even divulge different aspects. Every few minutes, for example when I was unable to find the way to say in good French what José Norberto Allende was saying in very good Spanish, I raised my eyes and looked at the photo; sometimes the woman would catch my eye, sometimes the boy, sometimes the pavement where a dry leaf had fallen admirably situated to heighten a lateral section. Then I rested a bit from my labors, and I enclosed myself again happily in that morning in which the photo was drenched, I recalled ironically the angry picture of the woman demanding I give her the photograph, the boy's pathetic and ridiculous flight, the entrance on the scene of the man with the white face. Basically, I was satisfied with myself; my part had not been too brilliant, and since the French have been given the gift of the sharp response, I did not see very well why I'd chosen to leave without a complete demonstration of the rights, privileges and prerogatives of citizens. The important thing, the really important thing was having helped the kid to escape in time (this in case my theorizing was correct, which was not sufficiently proven, but the running away itself seemed to show it so). Out of plain meddling, I had given him the opportunity finally to take advantage of his fright to do something useful; now he would be regretting it, feeling his honor impaired, his manhood diminished. That was better than the attentions of a woman capable of looking as she had looked at him on that island. Michel is something of a puritan at times, he believes that one should not seduce someone from a position of strength. In the last analysis, taking that photo had been a good act.

Well, it wasn't because of the good act that I looked at it between paragraphs while I was working. At that moment I didn't know the reason, the reason I had tacked the enlargement onto the wall; maybe all fatal acts happen that way, and that is the condition of their fulfillment. I don't think the almost-furtive trembling of the leaves on the tree alarmed me, I was working on a sentence and rounded it out successfully. Habits are like immense herbariums, in the end an enlargement of 32 x 28 looks like a movie screen, where, on the tip of the island, a woman is speaking with a boy and a tree is shaking its dry leaves over their heads.

But her hands were just too much. I had just translated: "In that case, the second key resides in the intrinsic nature of difficulties which societies . . ."—when I saw the woman's hand beginning to stir slowly, finger by finger. There was nothing left of me, a phrase in French which I would never have to finish, a typewriter on the floor, a chair that squeaked and shook, fog. The kid had ducked his head like boxers do when they've done all they can and are waiting for the final blow to fall; he had turned up the collar of his overcoat and seemed more a prisoner than ever, the perfect victim helping promote the catastrophe. Now the woman was talking into his ear, and her hand opened again to lay itself against his cheekbone, to caress and caress it, burning it, taking her time. The kid was less startled than he was suspicious, once or twice he poked his head over the woman's shoulder and she continued talking, saying something that made him look back every few minutes toward that area where Michel knew the car was parked and the man in the grey hat, carefully eliminated from the photo but present in the boy's eyes (how doubt that now) in the words of the woman, in the woman's hands, in the vicarious presence of the woman. When I saw the man come up, stop near them and look at them, his hands in his pockets and a stance somewhere between disgusted and demanding, the master who is about to whistle in his dog after a frolic in the square, I understood, if that was to understand, what had to happen now, what had to have happened then, what would have to happen at that moment, among these people, just where I had poked my nose in to upset an established order, interfering innocently in that which had not happened, but which was now going to happen, now was going to be fulfilled. And what I had imagined earlier was much less horrible than the reality, that woman, who was not there by herself, she was not caressing or propositioning or encouraging for her own pleasure, to lead the angel away with his tousled hair and play the tease with his terror and his eager grace. The real boss was waiting there, smiling petulantly, already certain of the business; he was not the first to send a woman in the vanguard, to bring him the prisoners manacled with flowers. The rest of it would be so simple, the car, some house or another, drinks, stimulating engravings, tardy tears, the awakening in hell. And there was nothing I could do, this time I could do absolutely nothing. My strength had been a photograph, that, there, where they were taking their revenge on me, demonstrating clearly what was going to happen. The photo had been taken, the time had run out, gone; we were so far from one another, the abusive act had certainly already taken place, the tears already shed, and the rest conjecture and sorrow. All at once the order was inverted, they were alive, moving, they were deciding and had decided, they were going to their future; and I on this side, prisoner of another time, in a room on the fifth floor, to not know who they were, that woman, that man, and that boy, to be only the lens of my camera, something fixed, rigid, incapable of intervention. It was horrible, their mocking me, deciding it before my impotent eye, mocking me, for the boy again was looking at the flour-faced clown and I had to accept the fact that he was going to say yes, that the proposition carried money with it or a gimmick, and I couldn't yell for him to run, or even open the road to him again with a new photo, a small and almost meek intervention which would ruin the framework of drool and perfume. Everything was going to resolve itself right there, at that moment; there was like an immense silence which had nothing to do with physical silence. It was stretching it out, setting itself up. I think I screamed, I screamed terribly, and that at that exact second I realized that I was beginning to move toward them, four inches, a step, another step, the tree swung its branches rhythmically in the foreground, a place where the railing was tarnished emerged from the frame, the woman's face turned toward me

as though surprised, was enlarging, and then I turned a bit, I mean
that the camera turned a little, and without losing sight of the woman,
I began to close in on the man who was looking at me with the black
holes he had in place of eyes, surprised and angered both, he looked,
wanting to nail me onto the air, and at that instant I happened to see
something like a large bird outside the focus that was flying in a single
swoop in front of the picture, and I leaned up against the wall of my
room and was happy because the boy had just managed to escape, I
saw him running off, in focus again, sprinting with his hair flying in
the wind, learning finally to fly across the island, to arrive at the footbridge, return to the city. For the second time he'd escaped them, for
the second time I was helping him to escape, returning him to his pre-
carious paradise. Out of breath, I stood in front of them; no need to
step closer, the game was played out. Of the woman you could see just
maybe a shoulder and a bit of the hair, brutally cut off by the frame of
the picture; but the man was directly center, his mouth half open, you
could see a shaking black tongue, and he lifted his hands slowly, bringing them into the foreground, an instant still in perfect focus, and then
all of him a lump that blotted out the island, the tree, and I shut my
eyes, I didn't want to see any more, and I covered my face and broke
into tears like an idiot.

Now there's a big white cloud, as on all these days, all this untellable
time. What remains to be said is always a cloud, two clouds, or long
hours of a sky perfectly clear, a very clean, clear rectangle tacked up
with pins on the wall of my room. That was what I saw when I opened
my eyes and dried them with my fingers: the clear sky, and then a cloud
that drifted in from the left, passed gracefully and slowly across and
disappeared on the right. And then another, and for a change sometimes, everything gets grey, all one enormous cloud, and suddenly the
spotches of rain cracking down, for a long spell you can see it raining
over the picture, like a spell of weeping reversed, and little by little,
the frame becomes clear, perhaps the sun comes out, and again the
clouds begin to come, two at a time, three at a time. And the pigeons
once in a while, and a sparrow or two.

From Cortázar to Antonioni:
Study of an Adaption
by HENRY FERNÁNDEZ

When one thinks of film adaptations of novels, the titles of classics come to mind: *War and Peace, The Grapes of Wrath, Ulysses*; or, at the more popular level, the titles of best-sellers: *Peyton Place, The Chapman Report, The Carpetbaggers*. In both cases the film maker takes no risks; the novel is a tried and true piece of fiction, either from a critical or a monetary point of view. What happens, however, when a modern, vanguard director decides to base a film on a work by an equally modern, vanguard writer? In the credits of Antonioni's *Blow-Up* the viewer is told that the film was inspired by a short story by Julio Cortázar. Both the Italian director and the Argentine writer, who are reported to be personal friends, belong to the same artistic "period," that of right now. Both receive more attention from reviewers than from scholars. Both are talked about in cocktail parties and hip college classes. Both are mature artists, yet their work promises to move in still new directions. Above all, both are creators of a sophisticated, self-conscious art. Therefore, the metamorphosis of story into film which we are about to consider will be of a special kind (a parallel would be if Eisenstein had adapted *Ulysses* and *if* we were studying it *then*, not now). Since I believe *Blow-Up* is a specific and unusual type of adaptation I have let my subject matter determine my method, that is, I will consider the problems of this particular adaptation without trying to either follow or prescribe rules for the study of film adaptation of fiction.

Before one even begins to examine the text and the film there are some obvious problems that must be considered. First, *Blow-Up* is a

From Film Heritage, *4 (Winter 1968–69): Copyright © 1969 by F. A. Macklin. Reprinted by permission of the author.*

full-length film while Cortázar's narrative is a short story. The conden-
sation observed in most adaptations from novels will obviously not be
needed; on the contrary, some expansion might be expected. On the
other hand, the film-maker might feel free to reproduce faithfully the
pace of the story at any given instance since he will not be pressed for
time. Secondly, the title of the short story is not *Blow-Up,* as in the
American translation, but "las babas del diablo," literally "The Devil's
Drool." More will be said about this later. Thirdly, the appearance of
Julio Cortázar's name on the screen means nothing to most American
moviegoers. Few of them will have read the story, so they will expect
nothing in the way of fidelity. Surely, this must be different in South
America, where Cortázar is very well known and read. However, if
Antonioni means to trigger any kind of association with the credit, this
is completely lost on American audiences. On the other hand, no
American reviewer compared the film to the story, a critical practice
which is usually a nuisance.

"Las babas del diablo" is found in a book called *Las armas secretas*
(*The Secret Weapons,* the title of one of the stories), first published in
1964. Like the other stories in the book, it takes place in Paris, where
Cortázar lives and where most of his narratives are set, not in swinging
London. As a matter of fact, Cortázar's Paris is far from swinging,
though it is quite bohemian. It is peopled by strange old men and
women, cats, students, artists, poets, mystics, and lovers, all in a desperate and often depressing search for another reality, playing a kind of
metaphysical hopscotch best seen in his novel *Rayuela.* Rather than the
guitar-busting, hard-rock sounds of the Yardbirds, it is the sound of
jazz that plays in Cortázar's fiction, listened to by devout groups in
small apartments or recording studios. The title "Las babas del diablo"
is a Spanish commonplace about being right in the devil's drool and
escaping before Satan closes his fangs, i.e., a close shave. The title is
important for it points to the morality-play nature of the main scene.
Like Antonioni's hero, the protagonist is a photographer. Like his
movie counterpart, he is idly walking around when he sees a couple
whose picture he snaps and later blows-up in his studio. The similarity
of plot ends here. There is no murder, no attempt to recover the film,
no theft of it. The couple the photographer sees—in a square, not a
park—is a very young man and an older woman. The photographer
conjectures that she is a prostitute making a pick-up and is glad to see
his picture-taking creates enough confusion to allow the embarrassed
boy to flee from the woman. However, there was a man sitting in a
parked car, who enters the scene during the argument between the
woman and the photographer. The latter cannot understand this man's

role until after the shots are blown-up and the realization that this was a homosexual pick-up becomes clear. Since the photographer is also the narrator the reader discovers the truth along with him. In a nightmarish scene, the photographer discovers that he, who by arresting time in his photograph saved the boy, must now live out the entire experience as the blown-up shot in his studio comes to life. The boy is saved again and the moving photographic image of the homosexual turns toward the photographer with open mouth. He too must experience the feeling of being right in the devil's drool before order can be restored.

The most important distinction between movie and story is that Michel, Cortázar's photographer, is also a writer, that is, he uses both the photographic and the written media. He makes this clear when he speaks of the two machines in the first paragraph, the camera and the typewriter. Michel spends about three pages explaining, or, rather, debating with himself, the reason for writing down this experience and the form he should use. Later, when he first finds the couple, he immediately begins to create a story around the *one* scene he sees. As the scene comes into clearer focus he alters the story to fit his new perception. He is both photographer and writer: he sees scenes, photographic scenes, which he paralyzes with his camera; while with his mind and with his typewriter he adds a temporal dimension to the scene. The two dimensions, spatial and temporal, collide in his studio when he observes the blown-up picture. He becomes immobilized, paralyzed in time, while the blow-up comes to life and acts out a narrative. Cortázar's theme is the tension between two media, one temporal and one spatial, and the tension between the man who uses these media and reality itself. Since reality moves along both dimensions without any boundaries between them, the man who dares to separate them, the man who invents and uses media, must suffer the consequences of such hubris. Michel thought the boy's fate was at stake and he felt satisfied to save him, while all the time it was he, Michel, who was playing the leading role. After being tormented by the images in his blow-up, the narrator sees only a sky with moving clouds in the photograph, a constantly fluid reality existing simultaneously in time and space, which he is content to merely sit and watch.

It will not be necessary to point out the obvious differences between story and film. I will just point out that since this is a full-length film there is enough time to develop the photographer's character more fully and to explore his relation to his environment, swinging London. The murder in the park, the girl's visit, the romp with the nymphets, the pot-party, the artist's mistress, all are extraneous to Cortázar's story. Yet, it seems, if only at first sight, that even the central theme of the film has little to do with the story, that Antonioni has merely taken a basic situation—photographer, couple, blow-up—from Cortázar and has created an entirely unrelated film.

In my interpretation, the nature of the two media and their relation form the theme of Cortázar's story. This is, I believe, also the theme of Antonioni's film. The key word is media, for film and story are different media, and any artist who uses his art as his theme knows enough about his medium to know he cannot *copy* a different art. The tension between photography and written narrative in Cortázar becomes a tension between photography and cinematography in Antonioni. While the latter's photographer is not a movie director, what he sees, that is, what the viewer sees, is a movie. This only becomes apparent when Antonioni makes him disappear at the end of the film, reminding the audience that this is a film and that there is someone at the other end of the camera. Nevertheless, though the presence of the moviemaker is not really felt until the end, there is, at least, the same tension between a fluid reality (narrative) and a static reality (photography) that we saw in the story. Yet, reality itself is larger than its representations in the media, for the protagonist, like a movie camera or a narrator, can only perceive part of it. However, like a movie camera, which can only record what it sees, and unlike a narrator, who can conjecture what lies beyond his perception, the photographer is left only with the knowledge of what he has seen: two lovers in the park. Thus, Antonioni's hero is taking the point of view of a movie camera, while Cortázar's is taking that of a narrator of fiction.

The key scene in both story and film is the blowing-up in the studio and the subsequent revelation. Antonioni has kept Cortázar's pace for this scene. The photographer blows-up his shots without knowing just why. He discovers, and the viewer discovers, what the blow-ups mean by a gradual process of involvement that becomes more frenzied until the moment of realization. Yet, there is a basic difference that stems from the fact that both story and film are about media and the media are different. In the story, the photographer blows-up *one* shot and it acquires movement; it becomes a narrative by coming to life. In the film, the photographer blows up several shots, then sections of these shots; still they reveal no secrets. Then, when the camera (the photographer's eyes) views a series of blow-ups in a particular sequence, a story unfolds. The photographer has dicovered montage. It is plain to imagine how clumsy and time-consuming this process would be on paper; lengthy descriptions of apparently disconnected minute details, and after that, the writer would have to explain the connection anyway. On the other hand, for a single blow-up to come to life in a film would be quite ludicrous, for, are we not watching a moving picture, after all? What would be so nightmarish about an animated photograph? The story narrates with words, the film with pictures. It is that simple.

The ending of *Blow-Up* is also related to the ending of the story in an analogous way. In "Las babas del diablo" the blow-up becomes a picture window to the sky, where clouds float in and out. The photographer accepts this, watches it, and tells it. The fact that he can no longer freeze reality, as symbolized by the constantly moving blow-up, does not disturb him. In *Blow-Up* the photographer picks up the invisible ball and throws it back to the players. The fact that this ball is a reality which he cannot see or photograph does not disturb him either. Both men have learned the limitations of their media and will now move in a world beyond the grasp of their cameras.

Perhaps some of the controversy which has sprung around *Blow-Up* would have been avoided if the reviewers had tried to see the film in its own terms. It is not a film about decadent, uninvolved, alienated, modern youth. *Blow-Up* is not *The Graduate*. It is not a rich, baroque film about film-making, like *8½*, although the illusion-reality problem is present in the movie. Both Cortázar's and Antonioni's protagonists say at some point in the respective works, "I am a photographer." Though this might not sound as impressive as saying "I am Hamlet the Dane" or "I am Lawrence of Arabia," it is certainly a statement which is pregnant with complexities, especially when one begins to wonder what photography is. Antonioni understood the resonance of such words. He also understood that Antonioni is a film-maker and Cortázar is a writer.

Index[1]

Agee, James, 28
Albee, Edward, 26, 38
Amiche, Le, 53
Animals, The, 7
Auden, W. H., 62
Avventura, L', 13, 14, 15, 16, 18, 20, 23, 43, 44, 53, 71, 77, 78, 79, 80, 81, 86, 95, 100, 106, 118, 126

Beatles, The, 89, 90
Beckett, Samuel, 26, 72, 73
Bellow, Saul, 71
Bergman, Ingmar, 4, 13, 37, 77, 90
Bianco e Nero, 90
Bogart, Humphrey, 95
Bond, Edward, 7, 45, 72
Borges, Jorge Luis, 26
Brown, N. O., 26

Cahiers du Cinéma, 28
Cameron, Ian, 13
Camus, Albert, 75
Cannes Film Festival, 2
Censorship in Denmark, 2
Cervantes, Miguel de, 127
Chabrol, Claude, 31
Chaplin, Charles, 33
Chaucer, Geoffrey, 125
Citizen Kane, 69
Clair, Jean, 6
Cocteau, Jean, 75

Coleman, John, 24
Contempt, 33
Corliss, Richard, 24
Cortázar, Julio, 3, 5, 6, 17, 18, 53, 72, 98, 99, 100, 113, 114
Crist, Judith, 27, 31
Crowther, Bosley, 2

Dante, 62, 119
Democritus, 114
Di Palma, Carlo, 7, 45
Dolce Vita, La, 70
Donner, Clive, 7
Don Quixote, 127
Dreyer, Carl, 31
Duvivier, Julien, 76

Eclipse, The (L'Eclisse), 13, 14, 17, 18, 20, 23, 26, 42, 60, 78, 86, 97, 100, 118
$8\frac{1}{2}$, 5, 14, 33, 38, 90, 119
Eisenstein, Sergei, 76, 117
Eliot, T. S., 54, 95
Esquire, 26

Fellini, Federico, 5, 14, 33, 35, 38, 54, 90, 119, 120, 127
Fitzgerald, F. Scott, 9
Ford, John, 31
Freccero, John, 6
French Can-Can, 33

---

[1] Index covers pp. 1–128 only and excludes references to Michelangelo Antonioni and *Blow-Up.*

Gambit, 31
Garis, Robert, 72
General, The, 3
Genesis, 114
Georgy Girl, 27
Gilman, Richard, 25
Giotto di Bondone, 59
Godard, Jean-Luc, 25, 31, 33, 76
Goldman, Annie, 102
Goldstein, Richard, 25, 27
Greene, Graham, 47
Grido, Il, 98, 105, 106, 126
Griffith, D. W., 69
Guerra, Tonino, 7, 45, 72

Haftmann, Werner, 59
Harris, Richard, 104
Hefner, Hugh, 97
Hemmings, David, 5, 7, 31, 32, 33,
    34, 36, 45, 47, 48, 49, 50, 51, 52,
    54, 60, 74, 78, 89, 98, 100, 107
Hernacki, Thomas, 105
Herzog, 71
Hiroshima, Mon Amour, 69
Hitchcock, Alfred, 1, 13, 14, 17, 19,
    24, 31, 33, 63, 67, 102
Hombre, 71
Homecoming, The, 73
How to Steal a Million, 71
Hudson Review, The, 26
Huston, John, 77

I Am Curious (Yellow), 2
Ibsen, Henrik, 4

James, Henry, 72, 79

Kael, Pauline, 25, 26, 27
Kallman, Chester, 62
Kauffmann, Stanley, 13, 26, 27
Keaton, Buster, 3
Keats, John, 90
Kinder, Marsha, 6
Kurosawa, Akira, 13

Lange, Dorothea, 55
Last Year at Marienbad, 3, 27
Lean, David, 77
Leigh, Janet, 14
Lennon, John, 89
Lewis, Jerry, 27
Limelight, 33
Lola Montes, 33
Look, 25
Losey, Joseph, 100

MacDonald, Dwight, 26, 28
Macklin, F. A., 105
McLuhan, Marshall, 26, 108, 116
Magic Mountain, The, 15
Magician, The, 37, 90
Mailer, Norman, 25
Mann, Thomas, 4
Manzoni, Alessandro, 126
Married Woman, A, 76
Marx, Karl, 122
Masaccio, Tommaso Guidi, 59
Metro-Goldwyn-Mayer Studios, 2, 8,
    33, 67
Miles, Sarah, 1, 7, 9, 24, 31, 33, 34,
    37, 45, 50, 75, 82
Mizoguchi, Kenji, 33
Modesty Blaise, 10
Morandi, Giovan Maria, 59
Moreau, Jeanne, 84
Morgan!, 27, 33
Morgenstern, Joseph, 24
Motion Picture Association of Amer-
    ica, 1, 2

Naked Night, The, 5
National Council of Churches, 69
National Review, The, 24
National Society of Film Critics, 2
New Republic, The, 26, 27
New Statesman, The, 24
Newsweek, 24
New Yorker, The, 25

No Exit, 94
Notte, La, 13, 14, 16, 17, 18, 20, 53, 78, 79, 80, 84, 95, 100, 102

Odyssey, The, 15
Open City, 69
Ophuls, Max, 33
Ottaviani, Cardinal, 97

Panofsky, Erwin, 3
Parsons, Talcott, 97
Persona, 5
Petrarch, 118
Pinter, Harold, 26, 31, 73
Pirandello, Luigi, 6, 19, 59
Plato, 114
Podhoretz, Norman, 25
Positif, 91
Promessi Sposi, 126
Proust, Marcel, 119
Psycho, 14
Pushkin, Aleksander, 117

Rake's Progress, The, 62
Rear Window, 17, 33, 63
Red Desert, The (Deserto Rosso), 7, 10, 13, 17, 26, 32, 33, 41, 45, 53, 59, 60, 61, 68, 73, 74, 78, 79, 80, 84, 95, 97, 102, 104, 118
Redgrave, Vanessa, 1, 5, 7, 19, 23, 31, 33, 34, 36, 45, 47, 48, 50, 55, 60, 76, 78, 84, 91, 108, 121
Reed, Rex, 27
Reisz, Karel, 34
Renoir, Jean, 33, 76
Ross, T. J., 6
Rosso, Giovanni, 59
Rouve, Pierre, 8

Samuels, C. T., 6
Sarris, Andrew, 116
Sartre, Jean Paul, 94, 122
Saved, 7
Sawdust and Tinsel, 5

Scott, James F., 6
Seastrom, Victor, 76
Servant, The, 100
Seventh Seal, The, 3
Shakespeare, William, 4, 81, 105
Shaw, George Bernard, 2
Sheed, Wilfrid, 26, 27
Simon, John, 18, 19, 24, 26, 27
Slover, George, 6
Snow, C. P., 112
Some People, 7
Sontag, Susan, 25
Steichen, Edward, 55
Stieglitz, Alfred, 55
Stravinsky, Igor, 62

Tempest, The, 4
Time Magazine, 24
Tiny Alice, 38
Tolstoi, Leo, 81
Troilus and Creseyde, 125
Truffaut, François, 32
TV Guide, 1

Uccello, Paolo, 60
Ugetsu, 33

Van Gogh, Vincent, 94
Variety, 28
Velasquez, Diego, 102
Vermeer, Jan, 102
Verushka, 125
Village Voice, The, 25
Vitti, Monica, 10, 78, 117

Waiting for Godot, 72, 73
Waste Land, The, 15, 54
When We the Dead Awaken, 4
Who's Afraid of Virginia Woolf?, 69

Yardbirds, The, 82, 83, 87
Yeats, William B., 4

Zabriskie Point, 98, 100, 103, 104

FILM FOCUS

Ronald Gottesman and Harry M. Geduld
General Editors

VOLUMES IN THE SERIES

Focus on Blow-Up
edited by Roy Huss

Focus on Chaplin
edited by Donald W. McCaffrey

Focus on Citizen Kane
edited by Ronald Gottesman

Focus on D. W. Griffith
edited by Harry M. Geduld